Santiago Pérez Triana
(1858–1916)

Colombian Man of Letters
and Crusader
for Hemispheric Unity

Santiago Pérez Triana

Santiago Pérez Triana
(1858–1916)

Colombian Man of Letters
and Crusader
for Hemispheric Unity

By
Jane M. Rausch
Professor Emerita, University of Massachusetts Amherst

Markus Wiener Publishers
Princeton

For information, write to: Markus Wiener Publishers
231 Nassau Street, Princeton, NJ 08542
www.markuswiener.com

Library of Congress Cataloging-in-Publication Data

Names: Rausch, Jane M., 1940- author.
Title: Santiago Perez Triana (1858-1916) : Colombian man of letters and
   crusader for hemispheric unity / Jane Rausch.
Description: Princeton, New Jersey : Markus Wiener Publishers, 2017. |
   Includes bibliographical references.
Identifiers: LCCN 2017005821| ISBN 9781558766242 (hardcover : alkaline paper)
   | ISBN 9781558766259 (paperback : alkaline paper)
Subjects: LCSH: Pâerez Triana, Santiago, 1858-1916. |
   Diplomats—Colombia--Biography. | Authors, Colombian—Biography. |
   Journalists—Colombia--Biography. | Businessmen—New York (State)—New
   York--Biography. | Businessmen—Colombia—Medellâin—Biography. |
   Colombia—Biography.
Classification: LCC F2276.5.P4 R38 2017 | DDC 986.106/2092 [B] —dc23
LC record available at https://lccn.loc.gov/2017005821

Markus Wiener Publishers books are printed in the United States of America
on acid-free paper and meet the guidelines for permanence and durability
of the Committee on Production Guidelines for Book Longevity of the
Council on Library Resources.

Contents

List of Images

Photos

Maps

Preface

In 1914 the editor of Bogotá's *El Tiempo Literary Supplement* wrote that it would be difficult to find a Colombian who was unfamiliar with the literary work of Santiago Pérez Triana. "His famous books *De Bogotá al Atlántico* and *Reminiscencias tudescas*, his eloquent political writing, his admirable articles, and his intense diplomatic activities over 30 years have made his name popular in countries that speak Spanish."[1] Two years later, the news of Pérez Triana's death announced in *El Tiempo,* the *New York Times*, *Hispania*, *El Gráfico* (Bogotá), and the *Times* (London) prompted an enormous sense of loss in Colombia. Several close colleagues wrote fulsome assessments of his career, describing him as a writer and journalist, and even more importantly, as a brilliant defender of so-called "weak" nations against U.S. and European aggression. They noted that when he was a Colombian delegate to the second Hague Peace Conference of 1907, his vigorous support for the Drago Doctrine brought applause from the other delegates and calls that he should be nominated for a Nobel Prize. Surpassing even this triumph was his leading role at the First Pan-American Financial Conference held in Washington, D.C. from May to July 1915. By that year he had become perhaps the best-known Latin American supporter for the Allies in the Great War, and his book, *Some Aspects of the War*, enjoyed wide circulation in the United States and Europe.

Fame, however, was fleeting. Despite Pérez Triana's celebrity in 1916, his role in Colombian and hemispheric history seems to have passed into oblivion 100 years after his death. Not even *El Tiempo* noted the centenary anniversary of his death in May 2016. Over the years his career has inspired only one slim biography—*Santiago Pérez Triana* by Sergio Elías Ortiz[2]—and yet the unique and fascinating trajectory of his life is worthy (as one commentator suggested) of a television series or a film.[3]

The son of Colombia's Radical Liberal President Santiago Pérez de Manosalbas, Pérez Triana lived most of his life outside of Colombia, first in the United States and later in Europe. His wife, Gertrude O'Day, who he married in 1896, was the daughter of Daniel O'Day, a wealthy North American manager of Standard Oil in France. His endeavors to succeed in commerce, first in the United States and then in Colombia, not only failed but also engendered serious scandals that forced him to flee both countries. In 1893–94 in an effort to avoid imprisonment by Colombian authorities, he slipped away from Bogotá, and with the aid of friends, crossed over the Eastern Andean Cordillera by a little-known route. After making his arduous way down the Meta, Vichada, and Orinoco rivers, he reached Trinidad in April 1894. He then immortalized this 90-day adventure in a book published in English as *Down the Orinoco in a Canoe*[4] and in Spanish as *De Bogotá al Atlántico por la via de los ríos Meta, Vichada y Orinoco.*[5]

Pérez Triana had an astonishing gift for languages. He was an attractive, convincing orator in English, Spanish, French, Italian and German. A prolific writer, he edited journals and published articles, essays, poems and even children's stories.[6] Although absent from Colombia for most of his adult life, he never stopped thinking of his distant country, so convulsed as it was by sterile revolutions. He opposed Rafael Nuñez's *Regeneración* (1877–89) and Rafael Reyes' virtual dictatorship (1902–07) but remained largely aloof from Colombian politics until the Panama Revolt of 1903. At that point he became actively engaged in opposing the treaties to establish Panamanian independence signed in Washington, D.C. in 1909 by Elihu Root for the United States, Enrique Cortés for Colombia, and Carlos Arosemena for Panama. His support of the Drago Doctrine at the second Hague Peace Convention and his numerous publications championing Latin America rights earned him an appointment as a Colombian delegate to the First Pan-American Financial Conference in 1915. He continued to be a forceful Latino voice supporting the Allied cause in the Great War until his death the following year.

The purpose of this biography, however, is not to write a film script based on Pérez Triana's varied experiences. It seeks only to restore his place in Colombian history by presenting a more extensive examination of his life, his career, and his impact on inter-American relations based upon a review of archival sources and his numerous publications. These voluminous materials can be accessed in Bogotá, through libraries in the United States, and also via inter-library loan. The catalogue of the Biblioteca Luis Angel Arango (BLAA) in Bogotá lists 60 of his publications which include various editions of his diplomatic documents, travel books, poems, and short prose known as *cuadros de costumbres*. The BLAA has a complete set of the *revista* (journal) *Hispania*, edited and published by Pérez Triana in London between 1912 and 1916—five volumes encompassing a total of 54 issues. Also at the BLAA are two manuscript collections: one consists of 56 letters Pérez wrote to his cousin Diego Mendoza Pérez between 1904 and 1916, and the other includes 13 letters to his nephew Jorge Lagos Mendoza, written between 1908 and 1913. Finally, the BLAA makes available essays describing his life and career that were published by his associates. I have supplemented this material with data extracted from the microfilmed U.S. Department of State Dispatches from United States Ministers—

roll 50, February 1–July 17, 1893 and roll 51, May 12, 1893–
August 25, 1894—and from contemporary newspapers including the *New York Times, El Tiempo,* and the *Times* of London.
Except where otherwise indicated, I am responsible for the
translation of his writings from Spanish to English.

Chapter One sets the scene by providing a brief overview
of Colombia's political situation after 1830 as well as background on Pérez Triana's parents, his early childhood, and his
education in New York City and at the University of Leipzig
in Germany. Chapter Two reviews his successes and failures
in commerce in New York City and Medellín. It also addresses
the allegations of corruption that forced him to flee Colombia.
Chapter Three discusses his marriage to Gertrude O'Day, the
daughter of a wealthy North American associate of John D.
Rockefeller, his varied activities in Madrid and London, and
his early publications. Chapter Four focuses on his political
opposition to Rafael Reyes' dictatorship (1902–09), and
sparked by his anger over the role of the United States in the
separation of Panama in 1903, his support of the Drago Doctrine while he was a delegate to the Second Hague Convention
in 1907. Chapter Five reviews his work for the Republic Union
government that replaced Reyes, his editing of a new journal,
Hispania, his support of the Pan-Americanization of the Monroe Doctrine, and his important participation at the First Pan-
American Financial Conference in 1915. Chapter Six looks at
his efforts to support the Allied cause in the Great War and the
months leading to his death on May 23, 1916 in London. The
conclusion in Chapter Seven assesses Pérez Triana's historical
importance at the turn of the twentieth century as a Colombian
man of letters and a crusader for hemispheric unity, and it suggests some reasons as to why he is almost entirely unnoticed
in Colombian history today.

As a matter of clarification, this biography deals with three generations of males all named Santiago Pérez. When there appears to be confusion as to which one I am referring, I have adopted the following system: the eldest Santiago and former president of Colombia will be referred to simply as Santiago Pérez or by his full last name, Pérez de Manosalbas. His son will be identified as Pérez Triana, while his grandson, Santiago, will be called by either of his two nicknames: Sonny or Santiaguito.

The book could not have been completed without the assistance of the Inter-Library Loan Department of the DuBois Library at the University of Massachusetts-Amherst and my able research assistant, Ingrid Natalia Ortiz Hernández, who scoured the Biblioteca Luis Angel Arango, the Biblioteca Nacional de Colombia, Archivo General de Colombia, and the Academia Colombiana de Historia, and sent photocopies of the more obscure materials related to Pérez Triana. I am grateful to Anthony Seidman for his fine translations of Pérez Triana's best-known poems, to Dr. Susan Berglund for her extensive research into the ancestry records of the Pérez de Manosalbas and Pérez Triana Family History, to Alexander López for preparing a helpful index, and to Sunna Juhn for her meticulous review of the text. Special thanks go to James D. Henderson who graciously agreed to read a draft of the manuscript and made many helpful suggestions. For any errors in the interpretation of the information, I of course am responsible.

1

The Land, the Times, and Young Santiago Pérez Triana, 1858–1883

*"The world belongs to those who seek
beyond the visible horizon."*
SANTIAGO PÉREZ TRIANA

Santiago Pérez Triana was born in Bogotá on September 15, 1858, the first child of the union between Santiago Pérez de Manosalbas and Tadea Triana. Before he died in London on May 23, 1916, he had witnessed Colombia's gradual shedding of its colonial past. A turbulent period of violent political strife between Conservatives and Liberals in the last half of the nineteenth century resulted in significant changes in the political, economic, and social structure of the nation. At times Pérez Triana was an active participant in these developments, and at other times he was keen observer, living abroad in Europe or the United States. After a brief examination of the geography, society, and political situation of Colombia in the second half of the nineteenth century, this chapter reviews Pérez Triana's experiences growing up as the son of a future president of the country.

Colombia in 1920

Colombia 1850–1920

It is commonplace to observe that Colombia is a country of varied regions. In addition to being the third largest country in South America in terms of territory, it occupies a strategic location with borders on the Pacific Ocean and the Caribbean Sea. Its geological core—three branches of the Andean Cordillera running north and south separated by the deep longitudinal valleys of the Cauca and Magdalena rivers—impose a rugged topography. From colonial times to the twentieth century, these Andean highlands, connected by the Magdalena River with the Caribbean ports of Cartagena and Barranquilla, dominated the country's development. They accounted for less than half the national territory of some 461,606 square miles, but encompassed 98 percent of the population.

Surrounding the Andean core are five lowland regions which remained largely outside the historical mainstream. First, lying east of the Andes are the Llanos Orientales, tropical grasslands that extend to the Arauca River and the Venezuelan border in the north and are bound to the south and east by the Guaviare and Orinoco rivers. To the south of the Guaviare River is the second region, Amazonia, a vast tropical forest that shares borders with Peru, Ecuador, and Brazil. Third, stretching along the Pacific coast is El Chocó, another area of tropical rain forest but traditionally more important from an economic point of view than Amazonia because of its mineral deposits of gold, silver, and platinum. Northeast of Barranquilla and jutting out to the Caribbean is the fourth region, the Guajira Peninsula populated since colonial times by the Guajiro Indians. Finally, there are the islands of San Andrés and Providencia, an archipelago located in the Caribbean 480 kilometers northwest of the Colombian coast.

Since all of Colombia lies within tropical latitudes, the Spanish, like the largest groups of Amerindians before them, preferred to live in the cool highlands of the Andes. By 1850, approximately 60 percent of the population of 2,243,730 lived in or around Bogotá, Tunja, and Socorro at altitudes of more than 7,000 feet in the altiplano of the Eastern Cordillera or along its western slope. Another 15 percent, including a high proportion of Afro-Colombians (recently freed from slavery by a law passed in 1851), inhabited the agricultural and pastoral areas of Popayán and the Cauca Valley or lived in the mining zone on the Pacific slopes of the Western Cordillera. The northern coastal region, including Panama and the seaports of Cartagena, Santa Marta, and Barranquilla, accounted for 15 percent of the people, while the remaining 9 percent lived in Antioquia, which was rich in minerals but poor in agriculture, forming a close-knit dynamic society nestled between the coast and the Cauca valley.[1]

In Pérez Triana's day, transportation between these regions was uncertain and hazardous. The roads were scarcely more than mule trails that pitched down the sides of steep mountain slopes at gradients only animals could negotiate. During the rainy season torrential storms frequently washed out whatever paths had been cut through the Andes, and on even the most important highway linking Bogotá to Honda on the Magdalena, "Mules sank to their girths in mud holes or skittered over slippery clay slopes."[2] Communication to the highland interior from the Caribbean coast depended on the Magdalena River. Boats poled by former black slaves took several weeks to make their way up 600 miles of the river's shifting channels to reach Honda. There passengers and freight transferred to mules for the long haul up the Eastern Cordillera to Bogotá or across the even more treacherous Western Cordillera to the Cauca Valley. By the 1850s the introduction of steamships greatly expedited travel along this route, but the trip remained costly and arduous throughout the nineteenth century.

Geographic isolation fostered the regional self-sufficiency that characterized the Colombian economy. Almost every region enjoyed variations in altitude within a closely circumscribed area and produced enough kinds of foods for a diversified diet. Each was more or less self-sufficient in agriculture, but some had assets that could be shared with the others: manufactured goods, flour, and textiles in the Eastern Cordillera; silver and gold in Cauca and Antioquia; and livestock in the coastal plains and the upper Magdalena. In the second half of the nineteenth century, tobacco followed by coffee emerged as viable export crops as the adoption of free-trade policies and the use of steamboats on the Magdalena lowered the cost of transporting these products to the exterior. In an equal manner, British manufactured goods and North American agricultural products began to infiltrate regional markets, limiting Colombian textile weavers and wheat growers in the highlands to production on a local subsistence basis. With some exceptions primarily around the *sabana* of Bogotá, agricultural and livestock methods were antiquated, scarcely varying from techniques introduced by the Spanish in the sixteenth century. Even by 1913, when four million cattle were pastured in the country's valleys and plains, there was still not a single meat packing house in the republic.[3]

By the middle of the nineteenth century, two parties—the Conservative and the Liberals—were vying for dominance of the national government. After a long period of Conservative rule, in 1849 the accession of José Hilario López to the presidency represented a break with the past. López ushered in a series of Liberal reforms including the abolition of slavery, decentralization of the nation's fiscal structure, and absolute freedom of the press. The Constitution of 1853 established the separation of church and state, allowed for civil marriage and divorce, extended suffrage to all male citizens over the age of 21, instituted popular election of governors, and weakened executive powers. Several years later, in the wake of the civil war of 1859–61, a final set of reforms privatized corporate properties for public sale and outlawed convents and monasteries. With the adoption of the Constitution of Rionegro in 1863, the extreme Liberal faction known as the Radicals reached the height of their power and managed to survive two coups d'état, the civil war of 1876–77, 12 rebellions, and six years of widespread agitation before losing control to the Conservatives in 1884. Despite continual military upheavals, this period, known as the Federation Era, saw the implementation of a national system of obligatory primary education, laid the basis for a commercial banking system, and promoted railway construction.

The election of Rafael Núñez in 1884, a successful Conservative uprising in 1885, and the adoption of the Constitution of 1886 brought about the defeat of the Radicals and placed the Conservatives firmly back in power. Centralism, strengthened institutional authority, and close church-state cooperation were the key elements of the new era known as *"Regeneración"* (Regeneration) that reversed some of the Liberal reforms to transform the country from a loosely bound association of regions into a nation-state.[4] Although weakened by factionalism and the forced exile of many of their leaders, the Liberals were not about to surrender their cause. Attempting to unify under a newly created political directorate—"Centro Liberal"—they nevertheless failed to defeat Rafael Núñez in the 1892 elections. Undeterred by the suppression of a short-lived uprising in 1895, during the next four years, the Liberals "moved inexorably toward armed revolt against *Regeneración*."[5]

The decade between 1899 and 1909 marked another turning point in Colombian history. The Liberals' armed fight against

the Conservatives known as the War of the Thousand Days
(1899–1903) was a ruinous conflict that ended in Conservative
victory but only after an estimated 100,000 men had died on
the battlefield or from disease, and thousands more were
maimed for life.[6] The conflict spawned the separation of
Panama from Colombia in 1903 and the dictatorship of Rafael
Reyes (1904–9) known as the *Quinquenio* which laid the economic and political basis for the consolidation of the modern
republic. Furthermore, it opened a period of strained relations
with the United States, which in its eagerness to build an inter-
ocean canal, openly abetted the Panamanians in their revolt
and later rejected demands by the Colombians to either apol-
ogize for this grievous diplomatic breech or to provide com-
pensation for Colombia's territorial loss.

Although Reyes was able to accomplish many useful reforms during his quasi-dictatorship, both Conservatives and
Liberals found his autocratic methods intolerable. For five
years he exiled or imprisoned critics who protested his policies
too loudly, but an unraveling financial system combined with
public outrage over his campaign to win approval of tripartite
treaties with the United States and Panama eventually brought
about his downfall. On June 13, 1909 the dictator abruptly resigned the presidency and sailed for Europe.[7]

The 21 years between 1909 and 1930 is known as the "Era
of National Harmony" or the "Conservative Republic." Although it began with a newly organized party—the "Republican Union," which included both Liberals and moderate
Conservatives—the disorganization of the Liberals enhanced
their rivals' domination so that after the 1914 election of José
Vicente Concha, Conservatives bolstered by the Catholic
Church were firmly in control. Despite repeated efforts to ratify a treaty with the United States that would allow Colombia
to recognize Panamanian independence and restore normal re-

lations with the "Colossus to the North," the outbreak of the Great European War postponed any serious negotiations on the part of the United States. This stalemate continued to be the case until the U.S. Senate, spurred by the prospect of oil exploration in Colombia, grudgingly ratified the Thomson-Urrutia Treaty in 1922.

Generations in Colombian History

In his *Generaciones colombianos,*[8] Abel Naranjo Villegas proposed a scheme for understanding the evolution of Colombian history during the nineteenth and twentieth centuries by dividing the ruling elite chronologically into seven different generations. In this context, a "generation," he explained, is a group of people who worked more or less simultaneously within the same social, cultural, and political contexts, even though their approaches to the phenomena of the time might have been quite different. Naranjo Villegas designated as the "Classic Generation" two groups of elites—those born between 1835 and 1850, and those born between 1850 and 1865—who determined the course of the nation from 1880 to 1905. The first group included, among others, Miguel Antonio Caro, Felipe Pérez, Jorge Holguín, José María Quijano Wallis, and Rafael Reyes. Representatives of the second group were Tomás Carrasquilla, Rafael Uribe Uribe, Baldomiro Sanín Cano, and Santiago Pérez Triana.

According to Naranjo Villegas, the Classic Generation lived in an era marked by authoritarianism and dogmatic and ideologically oriented thinking. Its members exhibited a sentimental attachment to Spanish culture and adopted an individualistic, egocentric approach to life. Although they did not adequately understand the confused reality of their country, they embraced a strict patriarchal style and two strikingly opposing political viewpoints reflected in the Radical Constitution of 1863 and the Conservative Constitution of 1886.[9]

Expanding on Naranjo Villegas's characterization of the Classic Generation, historian James Henderson adds that its members, having pursued law degrees, were well versed in Latin, Greek, and philosophy and spent much of their productive lives as teachers in schools they themselves had founded. They took for granted that they were born to lead Colombia at a time of astonishing change in the world. They strove to stay abreast of events unfolding in Europe, read the works of leading social theorists, and travelled to England, France, and Germany to study. Believing that progress in Colombia was inevitable, they recognized as their top priority the need to calm national passions to allow this progress to come about, and they especially looked to England as the country to emulate "for it was the home of the great Herbert Spencer and a model for less fortunate nations striving to begin their own process of industrialization."[10] As Pérez Triana belonged to the second division of the Classic Generation, his life reflects these characteristics to a large extent.

Naranjo describes the differences between the several nineteenth century generations, but Helen Delpar has pointed out that regardless of their birth date, "Colombia's Liberal leaders were linked to each other not only by political and economic bonds but also by kinship ties produced by intermarriage among members of prominent Liberal families."[11] These connections were likely to strengthen their political identity and make affiliation with Liberalism a part of the family tradition to be passed on to future generations and to preempt position of importance within the party. These ties, often spanning several generations, may be seen very clearly in the family of Santiago Pérez Triana. Of 40 Liberals appointed to a party advisory council in 1897, at least three were sons or nephews of older leaders: Diego Mendoza was a nephew of Santiago and Felipe Pérez and son-in-law of the latter; Eladio C. Gutiérrez was the son of Santos Gutiérrez; and José Camacho Carrizosa, nephew of Salvador Camacho Roldán, was also a member of the council.[12] By marrying a North American woman, Pérez Triana deviated from this tradition, but he still counted very much on the support of his uncles, Felipe Pérez and José Jerónimo Triana, his cousin Diego Mendoza, and his nephew Jorge Lagos. Such kinship ties reinforced his political identity.

Santiago Pérez Triana and his Family

The ancestors of the Pérez family arrived in the Spanish colony of New Granada during the conquest and eventually settled in the town of Zipaquirá. Pérez Triana's grandparents were Don Felipe Pérez Archila y Ortiz (1808–58) and Doña Rosa de Manos Alba del Castillo (1810–78). They were farmers who Sergio Ortiz described as *"cristianos viejos* of scant means but of good known lineage."[13] Pérez Triana's father, Santiago, was born to this couple on May 23, 1830 at Finca San José, while his uncles—Felipe and Rafael were born on September 8, 1836, at the Hacienda de Soconsuca in Sotaquirá, Boyacá, and on August 16, 1838 in Zipaquirá respectively. Despite their lowly birth, both of the two elder brothers—Santiago and Felipe—were destined to become significant figures in geographic studies, journalism, literature, and the Radical faction of the Liberal party.[14]

In the mid-nineteenth century most Liberal leaders had a similar educational background. They attended elementary schools near their homes and were later sent to Bogotá or to a regional capital for their secondary and professional education.[15] One of the best of these schools was Bogotá's

Colegio del Espíritu Santo founded in 1846 by Lorenzo María Lleras (1811–68). Santiago and Felipe Pérez came to the attention of Lleras when, as Director of Public Instruction, he oversaw examinations being held at the public school in Zipaquirá, where they were enrolled. Impressed by their abilities and recognizing that their parents were quite poor, Lleras decided to help the Pérez boys advance in their studies. Between 1842 and 1846 he taught them at the Colegio del Rosario in Bogotá, where he served as rector. After founding the Colegio del Espíritu Santo he arranged for their transfer to this new school where they both continued to excel. By 1848 Santiago, having manifested a remarkable ability in drama, poetry, and essay writing, was appointed professor of Spanish Language and Literature at the colegio. In 1850 he received the title of Doctor of Law and Political Science as did Felipe in 1851. Four years later on April 1, 1855 Felipe married Doña Susana Lleras Triana, daughter of Lorenzo María Lleras, an event that further strengthened the alliance between the two families.[16]

In the meantime, in 1852 Santiago Pérez was appointed as secretary of the Comisión Corográfica, a scientific endeavor that the government authorized in 1839 with the objective of exploring and charting New Granada's national territory and surveying its natural resources. Directed first by Colonel Agustín Codazzi and later by Manuel Ponce de León and Manuel María Paz, the commission members began their work in 1850. The group included native and foreign-born geographers, writers, and artists who produced maps, paintings, and written descriptions of the regions they explored. Botanist José Jerónimo Triana also accompanied the commission until 1851 during which time he collected over 2,200 specimens of herbal plants.[17] Santiago Pérez replaced Manuel Ancízar who resigned his post as secretary and published *Peregrinación de Alpha* in 1853, a descriptive account of the social conditions he observed during his travels with the expedition. Santiago Pérez continued Ancízar's work. He participated in the elaboration of the geographic studies and between 1853 and 1854 published his own observations as "Apuntes de Viaje por Antioquia y las provincias del sur" in two periodicals, *El Neogranadino* and *El Tiempo*.[18]

Despite this experience, Santiago never equaled his brother Felipe as a geographer. Felipe was not an original member of the commission, but on the death of Codazzi in February 1859, President Tomás Cipriano de Mosquera appointed him to prepare a volume compiling its findings. The result was his first important book, *Geografía física y política de los Estados Unidos de Colombia* published in 1862 and 1863.

Santiago Pérez, who was regarded as one of the most powerful intellects in Colombia, made his greatest literary contributions in the fields of poetry, essays, and philology. In 1851 he published *Jacobo Molai*, a play written in verse. Five years later in 1856, he published a second play, *El castillo de Berkeley*, and a *Compendio de gramática castellana por un granadino*—a manual intended for use in the public schools. He began a colegio that carried his name and served as Rector of the Universidad Nacional, which was established in 1867. In 1871, when the Academia Colombiana de la Lengua was created, he was elected as a founding member.[19]

In the 1850s, Santiago Pérez married Doña Tadea Triana, the sister of the botanist José Jerónimo Triana, a member of a distinguished Bogotá family. A daughter, Paulina Pérez Triana, was born in 1856, followed by Santiago Triana on September 15, 1858, and his siblings Eduardo, Amelia, and Eloisa.[20] Since Santiago Pérez and Tadea were teachers by vocation, they supervised their children's first letters and quickly realized that their eldest son showed a prodigious talent for learning. As a result, they enrolled Santiago Pérez at the Colegio de Pérez

Hermanos, an academy established by his father and his uncles, Felipe and Rafael. When that colegio was closed because its founders accepted government positions, Felipe Pérez resolved to reopen the old and well-respected Colegio del Espíritu Santo in 1867. Santiago transferred to that school where for three years he was one of the best students thanks to his great talents and dedication to his studies.[21]

In the meantime, Santiago Pérez de Manosalbas was deeply involved in Liberal politics. He supported the army led by Tomás Cipriano de Mosquera that defeated the Conservative forces of Mariano Ospina Rodríguez's government in the civil war of 1860–62 and was involved in the 1867 coup that unseated the dictatorial regime Mosquera later established. In that year he was elected to the Asamblea de Cundinamarca, and during the presidency of General Santos Acosta Gutiérrez, he became a member of the Senate. After Gutiérrez assumed the presidency on April 1, 1868, he appointed Pérez de Manosalbas Secretary of the Interior and Foreign Relations. Between June 22 and June 30, 1869, as "primer designado" he also served as president of the Republic during a brief absence of the general.[22]

Santiago Pérez Triana's teenage years were determined by his father's activities.[23] In 1870 Eustorgio Salgar, who succeeded Gutiérrez as president, named Pérez de Manosalbas Minister Plenipotentiary to the United States and charged him with the special mission of negotiating a Panama Canal treaty with President Ulysses S. Grant. Pérez de Manosalbas took young Pérez Triana along on this assignment and enrolled him in a New York City private school. Pérez Triana's studies in New York proved to be a pivotal experience, for it awakened his fascination with the cultures of foreign lands, and as Hernando Tellez has pointed out, this curiosity eventually led to his transformation into "ese tipo de colombiano de *dèraciné*" [that type of uprooted Colombian]. Pérez Triana would spend the better part of the following years living abroad because Germany, France, Spain, and especially England provided the environment necessary for his personal happiness and intellectual activity. While there is no doubt that he loved Colombia deeply and on many occasions served it effectively, life in Europe had an irresistible attraction for him offering adventure, business, intellectual activity, easy pleasures, good food, excellent wines, art museums, and the friendship of famous men. By contrast, Colombia after 1884 was a country ruled by a political regime he detested and a place that could provide only limited possibilities for his ambitious spirit.[24]

Pérez Triana remembered his studies at the New York school as being demanding, but because he learned English easily, he had no trouble making friends. Accompanied by a fellow Colombian student, he used to escape from the school on Sundays to attend operas in the city. The greatest obstacle to these escapades was his lack of pocket money, but at times some seats in the theaters were available at a very low price. Santiago had an excellent ear, and although he never learned to play an instrument, he became knowledgeable about music through his frequent attendance of operas, concerts, and musical events of all kinds. He also had a fine baritone voice, and in later life he used to sing in his office selections learned by heart from operas, Spanish songs, and French operettas for the delight of his friends.[25]

Santiago Pérez de Manosalbas continued as Colombian plenipotentiary to the United States for three years. In 1873, he returned to Bogotá while his son remained in New York. In that year he was elected to a two-year term as President of the United States of Colombia serving from April 1, 1874 to March 31, 1876. Just 44 years of age when he took office, he was already recognized as a writer of intellectual renown, vast

Santiago Pérez de Manosalbas

illustration, and cultivated talent. He was an active politician, and a hardworking public official who had risen up from lowly administration positions to become chief of state. As a private citizen he led an impeccable life. Described as a very quiet, retiring scholarly man, Pérez de Manosalbas, unlike many of his Liberal colleagues, was a practicing Catholic giving rise to Medardo Rivas's somewhat tongue-in-cheek declaration that his only liability for becoming president was the fact that he attended mass.[26]

In his inauguration address presented on April 1, 1874, Pérez de Manosalbas stated that while he understood that party differences still ran very deep, he urged the two parties to restrain their "militancy" so that "the Republic will be able to continue on its path of regeneration and improvement." He made clear that his principal goals were to consolidate national credit, promote material progress—especially railroads—and carry on the campaign for public education—all projects President Eustorgio Salgar had announced in 1870. Pledging to submit to the law and defer to public opinion, he expressed thanks for his elevation to the presidency and pledged to faithfully fulfill the expectations of those who had elected him.[27]

Among the five railroads that were under consideration, the Ferrocarril del Norte had top priority. Despite being a national undertaking that would unite Buenaventura on the Pacific coast with the lower Magdalena River by passing though the altiplanos of Cundinamarca and Boyacá, the project provoked heated debates. Pérez's opponents argued that the construction was too costly, that the nation should not invest funds in the public works of the states, and that there were not enough products available for the proposed railroad to carry to make it profitable. Overruling these objections, he approved a contract signed between Secretary of Hacienda, Aquileo Parra, and president of the railroad company, Joaquín Sarmiento, to complete the work within four years. In the meantime, efforts to continue implementation of the Organic Decree of November 1, 1870, which was an attempt to establish a national system of free public primary schools, provoked such violent opposition from the Conservatives and the Catholic Church that a new revolution against the government was simmering by the time Pérez handed over the presidency to his successor, Aquileo Parra Gómez in 1876.[28] The Radical Liberals who had believed that Pérez's ideas and actions would make him a symbol of peace and progress for Colombia, found to their regret that despite his many virtues, he lacked the tact, discretion, and flexibility necessary to be an effective political leader, flaws that explain the consensus of historians that his presidential term was largely unsuccessful.[29]

Once Parra had become president, he commissioned Pérez de Manosalbas to return to the United States, this time to buy arms to help the government win the war that began in 1876. In 1877 Pérez received a second commission: go to England to secure a loan to support railroad construction. By now his eldest daughter, Paulina, had married a German businessman named Essen and was living in the town of Elberfeld (today a part of the city Wuppertal) in North Rhine-Westphalia, Germany. As Pérez was planning his trip to Europe, he resolved that his son Santiago should accompany him and live with Paulina in Elberfeld in order to continue his university education.

Sojourn in Germany

The Germany that Pérez Triana would come to experience had only recently been reorganized by Otto von Bismarck in 1871 as the Second Reich (also known as Imperial Germany). With a population of 41 million, it consisted of 27 constituent territories, most of which were ruled by royal families. The nature of these territories was quite diverse, for they included six grand duchies, six duchies, seven principalities, three free Hanseatic cities, and one imperial territory. While the component states conserved autonomy for strictly local matters such as education, the imperial government dominated by the Kingdom of Prussia was responsible for military and foreign affairs and also exerted its authority in economic, social, and religious matters. After 1850 the country industrialized rapidly developing particular strengths in coal, iron (later steel), chemicals, and railways. In the space of a few decades, Imperial Germany became an industrial, technological, and scientific giant.

Under the German school system at the time, upon completing their elementary education, students attended *Gymnasium*—a nine-year prescribed course of study that included classes in Greek, Latin, religion, physics, philosophy, history, literature, math, and natural history. After the first year they attended an average of 34 hours of class per week in addition to being given home assignments. German teachers used strict rules and harsh measures to enforce discipline. The final objective of these efforts was to pass the *Abitur*, an exhausting examination that tested students in all subjects. After they successfully graduated from the *Gymnasium*, German students found the freedom offered by study in a university immensely appealing.[30]

Between 1870 and 1914 young people enrolled in one of 22 universities where they could major in one of four faculties: theology, law, medicine, or philosophy (what today would be considered liberal arts and sciences). Those who wished to study chemistry, engineering, mining, dentistry or architecture generally did so at one of the technical colleges (although Santiago majored in chemistry at Leipzig.) Most students finished their studies by passing a state examination in their chosen field. Some went on to conduct independent research and write a dissertation. Those who wished to teach at a university were required to write a second dissertation, the *Habilitation*. Upon obtaining these qualifications, the graduate enjoyed considerable status inside and outside Germany.

As pioneers of innovative scholarship, German universities were imitated across Europe and the New World. They attracted international scholars primarily on the basis of their excellence in research; however, the full freedom of student life provided an additional incentive. Because most courses required only a single cumulative exam at the end of the university year, a student had considerable freedom. With just three hours of lectures a day, a student could spend the rest of his/her time at the library or visiting museums. This schedule allowed some youths to avoid their classes altogether, but for self-motivated individuals such as Pérez Triana the freedom of student life provided an ideal opportunity to explore new fields and to develop their full potential.[31]

After joining his sister in Elberfeld in Germany, Santiago chose to enroll in the University of Leipzig located in the town of the same name 160 kilometers southwest of Berlin. Leipzig was the largest city in the federal state of Saxony with a population of some 125,000 in 1870. The university, one of the oldest in the world, had been founded in 1409. It grew slowly during the first three centuries of its existence, but by the 1870s it had become a world-class institution of higher education and research. With an enrollment of 3,000 students, it was a popular choice for international as well as German students as a way to further their education.[32]

Between 1877 and 1880 Pérez Triana studied physical chemistry at the University of Leipzig. Although he completed eight semesters, he did not receive the title of "Doctor" on leaving the university because he lacked knowledge of Latin, a requirement for the degree. This omission seems to have had little consequence, for as Ortiz notes, there was no better place than Europe and "especially the nation of such high culture as Germany to cultivate the splendid faculties of Pérez Triana, with all the means in his reach to occupy the intellectual position that later he would hold in the world."[33] The memories of this period in his life which he set down in a volume entitled *Reminiscencias tudescas* (German Reminiscences)[34] make clear that his five years in Germany were extraordinarily happy and that the impact of his experience enhanced both his understanding of the European world as well as what it meant to be Hispanic American.

Divided into seven short chapters entitled "Irma," "Otto," "Karl," "Hans," "Herrmann," "De Profesores," and "El Patent-Club," *Reminiscencias tudescas* suggests that while Santiago found the lectures and course work stimulating, he was especially impressed by the University's Conservatory of Music, which attracted students from all over the world. As someone with a strong appreciation of music, he was struck by the fact that music was an essential part of German family life, and that music and beer drinking were the hallmarks of student life at the university.[35] Another custom, the practice of dueling, he found less appealing and more difficult to understand.[36]

In the first chapter entitled "Irma," Pérez describes his friendship with a talented young pianist who was preparing for her final examination. Two days before she was to perform for her jury, the two decided to go ice skating on a frozen pool in a nearby park. As they were gliding along, Irma stumbled and in spite of Santiago's attempt to assist her, she fell and fractured her right hand. Distressed that she could not play for her final exam, Irma committed suicide by taking laudanum or some other kind of poison, but Pérez states that what killed her was the loss of her illusion or dream of becoming a musician.[37]

In "Otto," Pérez speaks of his encounter in Paris with a

young German student with whom he had developed a strong friendship while at the university. This chapter focuses on Otto's unfortunate love affair with another student, Helga, who eventually would marry Karl, but it also recalls the time Otto and Santiago shared in the laboratory where they worked together, and the long walks they used to take.

"Hans" is a portrait of a suave fencing professor Pérez visited, not for the purpose of taking lessons but to hear him recite ballads and songs. In this chapter he describes the fencing studio and the tradition of dueling. The students joined clubs where, in addition to drinking beer and singing songs, they practiced fencing. The leaders of these clubs encouraged duels between individuals. At the smallest perceived slight one student might challenge another, and the scars of these conflicts were regarded as a badge of honor. Hans had been a soldier, but coming from a musical family, he also loved to sing, and he explained to Pérez the important role music played in German families.

In the chapter titled "Karl," Pérez paints a picture of a young man who had embraced positivism but who was being pressured by his family to become a Lutheran pastor. He also describes the three types of associations students joined while at the University: the *Corpos*, *Burschenschafts*, and *Verbindungs*.[38] Each of these clubs had a special meeting room, and on one or two nights a week the members would hold official *Kneipes* or drinking bouts where those in attendance would down quantities of beer, smoke, and sing. "With the plasticity of youth," Pérez Triana writes, "the Spanish-American Society of Leipzig was formed, and its members celebrated *Kneipes* with as much fervor as if they were German and not natives of nearly all the Latin countries of America."[39] To join one had only to apply to the director of the group and provide proof that he was enrolled in the university. On the evenings of a *Kneipe,* each person contributed a portion to pay for the beer and rent of the meeting room. The members conversed in Spanish and presented speeches on different scientific or of literary subjects. In addition to Hispanic Americans, the group attracted Italians, Rumanians, Greeks, and even a few Germans who wanted to learn Spanish and found these meetings an excellent way to practice. German was the preferred language for singing, but the members also sang in Latin and introduced not a few Spanish, Cuban, Colombian, Venezuelan, and Mexican popular songs.[40]

"Hermann," (described in the fifth chapter), like Irma, was a student at the music conservatory, but, unlike Irma, he had already graduated as a pianist from the University of Munich and had come to Leipzig to earn an advanced degree as a Doctor of Music and Orchestra. Pérez describes in detail the music conservatory. Offering all forms of music instruction, it attracted even more foreign than German students, all of whom tended to live in the same section of the city, practicing their instruments and believing that they had a unique gift. Hermann was enamored with the music of Wagner, which was the substantial "food" of his spirit.

The chapter "De Profesores" describes Kolbe, a well-loved chemistry professor who introduced Pérez to the world of science. Kolbe had developed techniques for the industrial preparation of salicylic acid which was used to conserve all kinds of animal and vegetable-based foods. Pérez was fascinated by his lectures. He noted that the career of being a professor in a German university was an arduous and difficult task and that one must have great intellectual gifts and the tenacity and resistance of a diamond in order to succeed.[41] The professorship was like a priesthood but less holy because in the investigation of the truth, professors could not claim to be infallible. The chapter also explains that to be elected as the rector of a university was the crowning achievement of a professor's career, but notwithstanding the added prestige, it did not bring any increase in salary or special prerogatives.

In the final chapter Pérez explained that "El Patent-Club," like Topsy in *Uncle Tom's Cabin*, was never "born" but "just grew."[42] The 10 to 12 students who joined it got together twice weekly to drink beer and to read aloud classic German plays. They usually met in each other's houses, but sometimes when the weather permitted, they would go to a neighboring forest. There using torches for light, they would listen and discuss great national dramas, imagining characters such as Faust, Mephistopheles, Margarita, Phillip II, the Marquis de Posa, and William Tell. In this way, Pérez became familiar with the classics of European history.[43]

As *Reminiscencias tudescas* makes clear, Pérez's experiences in Germany affected him deeply. While he failed to achieve the title of "Doctor," he was saturated with Goethe, Schiller, Kant, and especially Heine and the music of Bach, Beethoven, and Liszt. As Nieto Caballero observes, "The Germany of beer, students, music, thinkers, legends and romantic ballads, clubs, simplicity, generosity and dreams—these were in his soul."[44]

In addition, Santiago took advantage of the time between semesters to travel around Europe. While in Paris he found a helpful mentor in his uncle, Don José Jerónimo Triana, his mother's brother mentioned earlier as the botanist for the Comisión Corográfica. Newly married, Don José had travelled to Paris in 1857 to continue his scientific work, and 10 years later he exhibited his collection at the Exposición Universal de Paris where he was awarded a gold medal and an object of art worth 5,000 francs. Don José initiated Santiago into the world of Paris and the beauty of French language and literature. With the aid of his uncle, he became acquainted with Paris academies, institutes and conservatories—all experiences that would serve him well in his later career.[45]

While living in Europe, Pérez honed his knowledge of several languages that he spoke and wrote with perfection, and he had met individuals of all races, ages, and customs. The difficulty was that when he left the University of Leipzig he had no fixed direction. He still had to resolve the problem of doing something in life, to pay his own expenses, to triumph over difficulties, and to demonstrate that he was not a failure.

One option was to rejoin his father. In 1877 Pérez de Manosalbas returned to Bogotá planning to dedicate himself to teaching and journalism. After his arrival, he became an active collaborator in Liberal periodicals such as *El Relator, El Tiempo, La Defensa,* and *El Mensajero.* In 1880 as an editor of *La Defensa* he began leading the opposition to Rafael Núñez, Colombia's president from 1880–82 and 1884–86. This type of political maneuvering, however, had little appeal to Pérez Triana, so that rather than returning to Bogotá, he decided to go back to New York City, this time to embark on a career in commerce and industry.

2

Success and Failure in the Commercial World, 1880–1894

"For the man of energy and good will, obstacles are the source of victory."

SANTIAGO PÉREZ TRIANA

Between 1880 and 1894, Pérez Triana embarked upon a career in commerce in New York City and Medellín. After achieving some initial success, his efforts created animosity in both cities and ended in failure and disappointment. They also led to what was perhaps the most exciting adventure of his life: a clandestine escape from his enemies in Bogotá via an arduous, uncharted route over the Andes and across the Llanos of Colombia and Venezuela. It was an unforgettable experience which he set down in a fascinating account that remains an important source for scholars who study Colombia's eastern territories.[1]

Pérez Triana in New York City

Pérez Triana arrived in New York in August 1880 and quickly secured a position of trust in a commercial firm managed by Miguel Camacho Roldán. During five years of employment he learned a great deal about how to conduct business, but his independent spirit encouraged him to strike out on his own. He decided to form his own commission office that would specialize in facilitating U.S. imports of products from Caribbean nations. In partnership with four other businessmen—Salomón Koppel, Charles Schloss, and Leopoldo and Enrique Pombo—Pérez Triana y Compañía began operations in 1885 in an office located at 16 Beaver Street.[2] The new firm soon developed a good reputation. Its trade was chiefly with Colombia and Venezuela in importing and exporting various articles of merchandise, but events occurring in Colombia during its first year raised a cloud over the company's operations.

Between 1880 and 1882, President Rafael Núñez, formerly a stalwart Liberal leader, began calling for "Regeneration" which he regarded as an inevitable phase in the maturation of Colombian Liberalism and involved deeper alliances with Conservatives. Promoting his ideas in newspaper articles, Núñez argued that the policies of previous Radical presidents who had dominated the national government since 1867 were responsible for the country's instability and had created a deadlock between the executive and the legislature. Despite opposition from other members of his party, he won reelection to a second term in 1884, a victory that proved to be the final blow to Liberal unity and culminated in the civil war of 1884–85.[3]

This short conflict began when Radicals in the state of Santander took up arms against the government accusing it of promoting electoral fraud. After mediation by the central government, the rebels agreed to a compromise in Santander but carried their grievances over the border to Boyacá. Hostilities soon broke out as well in Cundinamarca, Magdalena, Panama, and the coastal area dominated by Cartagena and Barranquilla where customs revenues were vital to government and rebels alike. By November 1884 the entire country was in revolt.[4]

Both Pérez Triana and Pérez de Manosalbas openly opposed President Núñez's alliance with the Conservatives. At the beginning of 1885, the new government began imprisoning members of the Radical opposition including Pérez de Manosalbas on the basis that they were supporting the insurgency. In February 1885 when General Ricardo Gaitán Obeso, the leader of the revolt on the Atlantic coast, sent Benjamín Gaitán to New York City to acquire arms and other war materials to support his army, it is not surprising that Gaitán solicited the services of the Pérez Triana y Compañía. He deposited with the firm $30,000 in letters of exchange with Europe and later $33,000 in American dollars. Subsequently the account grew to $88,000. Pérez Triana bought on commission rifles, ammunition, machine guns, and uniforms in sufficient quantity to equip a division of 2,000 men which he dispatched to Barranquilla on the ship *City of Mexico*. The *City of Mexico* reached its destination although the Colombian government later sanctioned its captain for taking part in clandestine activities.[5]

Pérez Triana y Compañía charged a commission of five percent or twice the usual amount for sourcing and shipping the arms. Even after the funds furnished by the revolutionaries were exhausted, the firm continued to provide Benjamín Gaitán with $12,146.75—a sum that enabled him to buy the steamship *Aden* which embarked for Colombia carrying 1,000 Peabody rifles, 100,000 bullets, 500 belts, 48 cornets and 12 drums. Pérez Triana borrowed the funds from a Mr. Williams Jr., a New York businessman, pledging the ship and its contents as collateral to cover the risk.[6]

Yet Núñez's government forces crushed General Ricardo Gaitán's revolt in September 1885 before the ship reached Colombia. Benjamín Gaitán, still in New York, was devastated for he was liable for the $12,147 debt. When he asked Pérez to take charge of the ship and arms and forgive the debt, Pérez refused. Gaitán then accused Pérez of illegally doubling his commission, of deception regarding the value of the ship *Aden,* and of profiteering on other articles. Pérez denied these charges, but the upshot was that Gaitán presented himself to Dr. Clímaco Calderón, the Colombian consul in New York City, to ask for amnesty and a safe conduct certificate in order to return to Colombia. Gaitán agreed to hand over to the government the *Aden* and the war material that was pledged to Mr. Williams for more that $12,000. On this basis, Calderón allowed Gaitán to return to Colombia on November 10, 1885. This agreement also exonerated Pérez Triana of the assertion that he had illegally doubled his commission, but he remained responsible for the expenses of defending the captain of the *City of Mexico,* who was being held in Washington, D.C. on charges of "acts of hostility and piracy against a friendly power." Although the captain was liable to a fine of $10,000 and 10 years in prison, Pérez was able to arrange for his freedom.[7]

While his firm was dealing with this crisis, Santiago had also begun his literary career by editing a journal called *La America.* In early 1885 he received a visit from twenty-one-year-old Eduardo Zuleta Gaviria who had just received a doctorate in medicine and surgery in Bogotá and had travelled to New York City to attend Columbia University. Zuleta went to Pérez Triana & Co for a bill of exchange. Pérez greeted him cordially and agreed to cover his request. Zuleta recorded his first impression of the entrepreneur in his "Elogio de Don Santiago Pérez Triana" which he read at a meeting of the Academia de la Lengua Colombiana on August 6, 1919. He recalled Pérez Triana then 27 years old, as a man "in full youth…short, fat, myopic, smiling, and nervous."[8] While he and Pérez were talking in the latter's office, employees of the firm came and went, and Pérez gave orders in German, English, and Spanish. After Pérez had granted Zuleta's request, he invited him to lunch at a neighboring restaurant in order that he might meet the Cuban revolutionary, José Martí. According to Zuleta, at this time Pérez Triana was living the "life of a prince." Numerous guests came to his house which was the center for many friendships. He was received with honor in the homes of men of letters. His prodigious memory surprised everyone. He was familiar with outstanding authors from Mexico to Patagonia and could recite poems written by Longfellow, Whittier, Pombo, Fallon, Musset, Hugo, Tennyson, Swinburne, Núñez de Arce, Campoamore, Heine, and Goethe. He circulated at his own expense a beautiful edition of the famous translation of Edgar Allan Poe's *Raven* by the Venezuelan poet Juan Pérez Bonalde.[9]

In contrast to Santiago's flourishing cultural activities, Pérez Triana & Co failed to prosper. The difficulty lay not so much with the entrepreneur's lack of ability but with the slow recovery from the U.S. economic depression of the 1870s. Limited capital and the contraction of credit paralyzed his business ventures. By February 1890 Pérez Triana was forced to declare bankruptcy, and to avoid meeting the demands of his creditors, he made hasty preparations to leave the United States. On May 6 his application to become a naturalized U.S. citizen was approved, and shortly afterwards he abruptly left New York City traveling on a U.S. passport.[10] His departure was none too soon for on May 27, Judge Lawrence of the New York Supreme Court placed an attachment for $191,431 on the insolvent firm in favor of the Western National Bank.[11]

Pérez Triana planned to establish a business in Medellín, the capital of the department of Antioquia in Colombia, but his itinerary had a stopover in Havana, and a French comic opera company was performing there. Spurred by his great love of music, Santiago stayed to attend its performances every night and quickly befriended the director. When the company ended its season in Havana and prepared to set off for Mexico, Pérez

Triana decided to accompany them. On reaching Vera Cruz the company's director announced that their first performance would be an opera by Offenbach, but after the group arrived in Mexico City, the unforeseen death of the second tenor set off a frantic search for a replacement. When no substitute could be found, Pérez Triana offered to take the role, and the director agreed being aware of his impressive singing abilities. As a result Santiago became the first Colombian, under an assumed name, to perform in a composition by Offenbach before a Mexican audience.[12]

While in Mexico City Pérez Triana attempted to use his connections with friends in Europe and America to finance railroads, electric plants, and loans for Mexico, El Salvador, Venezuela. His contacts, however, were reluctant to partner with the dictatorial Mexican government of Porfirio Díaz, and the environment in El Salvador and Venezuela was no better. Given this situation, Pérez Triana decided to continue on to Medellín where efforts to build railways were well underway.

The Financier in Medellín

After arriving safely in Medellín in late 1890, Pérez immediately began to rebuild his reputation as a financier by publicly defending his actions in New York City. In a long document, *La Casa de Pérez Triana & Cia a sus relacionados*,[13] he blamed his associate Enrique Pombo for the problems incurred by his firm, but this argument did little to reconcile his U.S. creditors.[14] Having formed a favorable concept of Antioqueñan businessmen, he developed friendships with Fidel Cano, Luis E. Villegas, and Pedro Nel Ospina and was soon active in commercial ventures.[15] Of special interest was the Ferrocarril de Antioquia which had been initiated in 1874 during his father's presidency through a contract with the Cuban entrepreneur,

Francisco J. Cisneros. Cisneros' plan was to unite Medellín by rail with Puerto Berrío on the Magdalena River following the natural courses of the Nus and Porce rivers in order to avoid geographical obstacles posed by the Cordillera Occidental which effectively blocked land transport from the city to the river. Unfortunately, the war of 1885 forced the suspension of railroad construction leaving Cisneros as the principal creditor of the national debt. In spite of having lost the railroad contract, his financial situation was secure because British legal protection ensured his London-registered companies and associates would be repaid by the Colombian government.[16] In 1888 the government signed a new contract with the North American engineer Charles S. Brown, but Brown was equally unsuccessful in completing the work.

There was little progress until Baltasar Botero Uribe became governor of Antioquia in 1890. In that year Congress called for a new contract in which the national government and the department would each pledge 50 percent of the financial support needed for the railroad's completion.[17] Several companies competed for the contract, and in July 1891 it was finally awarded to a group of North American engineers, led by Anthony Jones who promised to finish the work in fourteen months.[18] Construction began, and the route advanced toward Medellín before it was blocked by the obstacles posed by La Quiebra Mountain and the need for additional funds to the tune of 5,165,000 pesos.[19]

In the meantime, the government had decided to dispatch Alejandro Barrientos to London to get a loan to support the railroad. Barrientos, lacking familiarity with European business people, solicited the aid of Santiago Pérez Triana not only because he knew French, English, and German but also because of his experience in merchant and industrial enterprises.[20]

The two men started off in May 1891 with 1,000 pounds sterling for expenses. Their original plan was to go to London, but for some unexplained reason they remained in France where they began negotiations with A. Desprez & Company based in Paris, De Grelle Houdret & Company of Brussels, and the Krupp company of Essen, Germany. Progress was slow, and Barrientos decided to travel to Spain leaving Pérez Triana in charge of finalizing the loan. Armed with sole power, Pérez Triana, using all his skill, managed to persuade De Grelle Houdret & Company to take charge, under an arrangement in which he would receive a commission if his services proved satisfactory. De Grelle recommended that he open negotiations with the British company Punchard, McTaggart & Lowther. Accordingly, Pérez went to London and convinced Punchard to make the loan for the construction of the Antioquia railroad. The firm promised that once the Antioqueñan government approved the agreement, Pérez would receive a three percent commission of its value to be divided equally between him and the intermediaries De Grelle Houdret & Company.[21]

On returning to Colombia in the company of Mr. William Ridley, a representative of Punchard, Pérez Triana and Barrientos concerned themselves with creating a favorable atmosphere for the ratification of the contract by the national government and the Department of Antioquia. Pérez Triana stopped in Cartagena on his way to Bogotá hoping to win the approval of President Rafael Núñez, who was then residing in that city. Núñez granted him a three-hour interview. After hearing the details of the contract, he indicated his support and promised to write to Governor Abraham García encouraging him to accept the deal.[22]

By the beginning of 1892, Pérez Triana was back in Medellín campaigning with articles published in two periodicals urging the departmental assembly to ratify the contract. The strongest opposition to the measure came from the *Junta Asesora* (advisory committee) of the railroad project, and on August 8, 1892, the Antioquia Assembly voted to refer the right to approve or disapprove the measure to this committee. The Junta strongly objected to the 3 percent commission granted to Pérez Triana and De Grelle Houdret & Company if the Punchard, McTaggart & Lowther contract was approved. It recommended that the arrangement be rejected, but rather than accepting the Junta's advice, Governor García took the unusual step of closing the Assembly.[23] The departmental government then negotiated with William Ridley for a more acceptable version of the Punchard, McTaggart & Lowther contract for construction and loans. An agreement was reached on September 24, 1892 and signed into law by Governor García on the same day. At the signing ceremony Pérez Triana, who was regarded as the principal promoter of the deal, publicly affirmed that the advantages it offered far outweighed any legal technical or economic inconveniences.[24]

Since the national government also had to approve the contract, Governor García charged Baltasar Botero, Jorge Bravo, and Pérez Triana with its defense in Bogotá. After an absence of some fifteen years, Pérez received a joyous greeting from his family and friends in the capital. Taking a house on Carrera 6 between Calles 13 and 14, he called together several acquaintances to discuss the publication of a new *revista* (journal). Included in this group was Baldomiro Sanín Cano who met Santiago for the first time. In his memoir, he noted that Pérez had a complete understanding of the qualities of the modern *revista* he wanted to begin, but that the times were not propitious for the launching of such a publication.[25]

Although Rafael Núñez won reelection as president in February 1892, he remained in Cartagena, leaving Vice President Miguel Antonio Caro in charge of the government. With *Re-*

generación in full force, Radical Liberals faced suspicion and jealousy and were under constant attack. Beginning in October 1892 an atmosphere of hostility began to surround Pérez Triana's commercial efforts. Vice President Caro refused to receive him to discuss approval of the Punchard, McTaggart & Lowther agreement since the British company was also raising new reservations. The Antioquia Assembly threatened a legal investigation into Pérez's handling of the contract arguing that he had "illegally" taken on the leadership role that it had subsequently assigned to Juan Pablo Gómez for negotiating the final contract.

On February 27, 1893 former President Santiago Pérez de Manosalbas, a fierce opponent of Núñez, resumed publication of *El Relator* and the directorship of the Radical party. Having been absent from Colombia during the previous fifteen years, Pérez Triana, unlike his father, had not been involved in Liberal politics. Given the circumstances, he sympathized but did not actually support Pérez de Manosalbas' efforts. The Radical opposition to the Núñez-Caro regime, led for the most part by military men, saw war as the only way to end *Regeneración* and to restore the Rionegro Constitution of 1863. Pérez de Manosalbas preferred to trust in the powers of the press and legislature rather than to foment a war that would bring only desolation, ruin, and discredit to the nation. Meanwhile the government, anxious to consolidate its power, was alert to any rumor of armed protest.[26]

In this situation of increasing insecurity, Pérez Triana began making plans in March to travel to Europe to continue negotiations with Punchard, McTaggart & Lowther, but on April 1 he received a communication from Minister of War General Antonio Cuervo that he would not be allowed to leave Bogotá until he could justify the object of his trip. He immediately met with Cuervo who demanded assurances that the nature of his proposed journey was commercial, that it would contribute to the promotion of public peace, and that Pérez would submit proof of his authority to work on behalf of the contract with Punchard, McTaggart & Lowther. On April 10, Pérez delivered the requested documents. Cuervo told him that he would send them on to the vice president and would tell him of Caro's decision. During the next few days several individuals friendly to the government urged Caro to allow Pérez Triana to leave, but the vice president remained reluctant to grant permission for him to do so.

Concerned that authorization would be denied, Pérez decided to play his ace card. On April 19 he wrote to John T. Abbott, the head of the U.S. legation in Bogotá, stating that although he was Colombian by birth, he had been a naturalized U.S. citizen since 1890. He explained he was planning the trip in order to return to the United States via Europe and that his detention in Bogotá was simply a means of retaliation because of the anti-government writings of his father with which he had nothing to do and over which he had no control. As a U.S. citizen Pérez demanded the protection of the American government "against this gross injustice" to which he had been submitted.[27]

Sympathetic to Pérez's situation, Abbott agreed to advocate with Caro on his behalf. He warned Pérez to refrain from publicizing his U.S. citizenship and to act with moderation. Because he suspected that the real reason for Pérez's trip was to obtain arms for the Liberals from abroad, Caro proved resistant to Abbott's appeal. At that point, Abbott via a "mutual and discrete friend" informed Caro that since Pérez Triana was a citizen of the United States, he was reviewing his detention in Colombia in order to consult the U.S. government about the case. This strategy appeared to work, for on April 22 Pérez Triana received a letter from Cuervo permitting him to leave

Colombia in order to pursue his business with Punchard.[28]

Despite receiving this permission, Pérez Triana continued to delay his trip. When the new U.S. minister to Colombia Luther F. McKinney arrived in Bogotá in July to take over the leadership of the legation from Abbot, the latter explained to him that Pérez was still in the city but was preparing to depart. In fact, Pérez Triana was making final arrangements to leave on August 7, when news of a Liberal conspiracy in Barranquilla provoked Vice President Caro to adopt drastic measures. On August 4 he shut down *El Relator*, the principal Radical Liberal newspaper, and confiscated its press. After arresting its editor, Pérez de Manosalbas, and seizing all his papers, he ordered him to leave Colombia within the next 18 hours. Unfortunately, the impounded documents included papers belonging to Pérez Triana pertaining to his business in Europe and America that were in his father's house, although his name did not appear in any reports of the supposed anti-government plot. Since it was impossible for him to leave Colombia without these papers and letters, Pérez Triana requested that they be returned to him. After examining him about the situation for four hours, the Minister of Justice informed Vice President Caro that he was convinced Pérez Triana was not implicated in the Radical conspiracy and that he should be allowed to leave the country. Vice President Caro agreed. Once the vital papers belonging to Pérez were returned to him, he left Bogotá on September 13 intending to travel to the coast via riverboat down the Magdalena.

Armed with an official Colombian passport he arrived in Honda on September 15, but the following day local authorities, acting on an order from the Ministry of Justice, arrested and confined him in the local jail—the "Ciega de Honda"— considered one of the vilest prisons in Colombia. Yellow fever was endemic to Honda, and the "Ciega de Honda" lacked ventilation and the most elemental resources of modern hygiene. Francisco Sanín Cano, a lawyer vacationing in Honda, learned of Pérez Triana's plight and believed his imprisonment in the "Ciega de Honda" was a veritable death sentence. Francisco alerted his brother Baldomiro who lived in Bogotá of the situation, but despite the latter's intercession, Bogotá authorities refused to intervene.[29]

At this point Francisco suggested that Santiago could gain his freedom by claiming his status as a U.S. citizen. Pérez Triana quickly agreed, and Francisco sent a telegram to Luther F. McKinney in Bogotá informing him that a U.S. citizen being detained in a pestilential prison in Honda was in danger of succumbing to yellow fever.[30] McKinney, fully aware of Pérez Triana's dual citizenship acted immediately to demand that he be transferred to Bogotá. He spoke first with Vice President Caro who said that he had not ordered his arrest, but that the request had come from Medellín, where authorities believed that some documents Pérez was carrying would expose department officials guilty of bribery in the Punchard, McTaggart & Lowther contract.

McKinney then exchanged a series of notes with Foreign Minister Marco Fidel Suárez who believed that Pérez was guilty of bribing the officials and questioned the authenticity of his U.S. citizenship. Suárez pointed out that Pérez Triana had left New York City in 1890 under a cloud, but the American minister held firm that he was a bona fide U.S. citizen. Further, he maintained that if Pérez was guilty of a crime, the Minister of Justice should present specific charges according to the laws of the country. Apparently the Antioqueñan government had produced papers informing Suárez of their suspicions, but they failed to issue formal charges. McKinney maintained that it was an injustice to keep an American citizen prisoner indefinitely and without charge. If certain high officials were guilty of accepting bribes and were not being prosecuted, it was wrong to punish Pérez where there was no proof of his having offered them bribes. As a representative of American interests, it was McKinney's duty to see that an American citizen should not suffer for the sins of others and that he should at least have the benefits of the laws of the land. After threatening to bring the issue to the attention of the secretary of state in Washington, McKinney succeeded in getting Pérez Triana transferred to Bogotá in early December, where he was released on bail of $1,000 with orders to appear in Medellín when the courts demanded his presence. To explain his actions in the matter to U.S. Secretary of State Walter Q. Gresham, McKinney sent a letter dated January 12, 1894, reviewing the entire episode. He concluded: "I give it as my candid judgment, and it is the judgment of the public here, that the Government had no intention of trying Mr. Pérez, but their only purpose was to prevent his leaving the country, fearing he may, with his father who is in Europe, assist the Liberal Party here in revolutionary acts, although it is a fact that Pérez has never taken any part in political matters."[31]

Pérez Triana was now free on bail, but there was no doubt that the government had every intention of eventually sending him to Medellín to be tried for bribery. Given this perilous status, with the help of his friends and family he began preparations to leave Colombia clandestinely as soon as possible.[32] Starting from a hacienda situated in northern Cundinamarca, he resolved to avoid the Magdalena River and to flee the country via a seldom used route though the Colombian and Venezuela Llanos—a region virtually unknown at the time.

Down the Orinoco in a Canoe:
Pérez Triana's escape from Colombia

On December 21, 1893, Pérez Triana accompanied by his servant, Fermín, and a friend, Alex, left Chocontá, Cundinamarca to embark upon a four-month journey eastward over the vast plains. His objective was to arrive at Ciudad Bolívar, Venezuela, located in the delta of the Orinoco River by late April 1894. It was to be an odyssey that he would subsequently document in a book published first in Spanish as *De Bogotá al Atlántico por la vía de los ríos Meta, Vichada y Orinoco* in Paris in 1897 and in 1902 in a modified English version entitled *Down the Orinoco in a Canoe.*[33]

Traveling from Cundinamarca at an altitude of about 8,500 feet, the trio began their great adventure by riding on horseback for seventeen hours to reach the hacienda of Gambita, where another friend, Raoul (who had gone ahead to prepare everything for their long journey), was waiting. At this point the expedition took on something of an aspect of a caravan. Besides Alex, Raoul, Santiago, and Fermin, there were four muleteers and ten or twelve mules laden with luggage, tents, provisions, and other paraphernalia.[34] Santiago noted: "This mob of travelers was so unusual that the simple folks in the villages through which we passed said that his lordship the archbishop was no doubt on tour. On hearing this and finding that the people began to kneel by the roadside, rather than shatter their illusion, I—knowing that I was the most episcopal-looking of our crowd—decided to give my blessing, which I did with due unction to the kneeling maidens and patrons along the roadside."[35]

The group travelled eastward with the goal of reaching the Meta River, one of the largest tributaries of the Orinoco. After three days' ride they arrived at the estate of a friend near the town of Miraflores. Here they prepared for the last stage of the land journey, which would take them through the dense forest of the lower eastern slope of the Cordillera and bring them to the edge of the tropical plains and the rivers whose tributaries flowed eastward toward the Orinoco. The descent proved to be quite steep. At times the travelers got down from their mules, walking on foot behind the guides to surmount huge boulders and tree trunks. After toiling for five days, they had their first glimpse of the Llanos—seemingly endless grasslands where the sun shone on ribbons of silver streams and copses of *moriche* palms. Within a few hours they reached the hamlet of San Pedro del Tua, a cattle trading station, where traders and breeders met at certain times of the year. On New Year's Day, January 1, 1894 they completed the first stage of their journey.[36]

The mayor of San Pedro del Tua allowed the travelers to stay for the night in his own house. He calmly accepted their claim that they had come to purchase land in the Llanos (an obvious fiction since grazing land belonged to all; individuals did not own land but merely "squatted" on parcels wherever they liked). Once the travelers revealed that their true goal was to reach Venezuela, the mayor whose name was Higinio Leal suggested that he go with them since he knew the way.

The travelers quickly accepted his offer. They were bringing along an enormous collection of supplies that included eight cases of food, six large jugs of *aguardiente*, and a half a ton of salt—a product highly valued in that region which they planned to use for bartering. They also had a box of books, trunks carrying clothing, and an arsenal consisting of four fowling pieces, six Remington rifles, two Spencer rifles, ammunition, one dozen machetes, and four revolvers. Leal suggested that their trip would be easier if they jettisoned half of this stuff, but the travelers insisted that they wanted to hang on to it as long as it was feasible. Leal's plan was to follow the Río Tua by canoe to the Meta River, but once reaching the Meta they would need to find larger canoes to take them on to the Orinoco. When they arrived at a village called Urbana, they would find even larger craft to take them to Caicara where they might wait for the steamship that regularly sailed to Ciudad Bolívar. According to Leal, this part of the journey, barring unforeseen accidents, would take about fifty days.

On arriving at the banks of the Rio Tua, Pérez Triana, Alex, Raoul and Fermín (who quickly proved adaptable serving as a muleteer, valet and cook) found canoes which were to be paddled by seventeen *peones* hired by Leal. Pérez commented that these canoes "were so small that we were packed like herrings, but, as it was impossible to obtain others, we had to make the best of them."[37]

The river phase of the trip began at 6:00 a.m. on January 3. Canoe travel proved difficult, for the waters were shallow due to the dry season, and the men frequently had to get out of the boats so that they could portage them over the land. By 5:00 p.m. they stopped for the day and camped in the open along the river shore. By the time they reached the Meta, the rhythm of the days had fallen into a predictable pattern. Leal woke the party at 3:00 a.m. Between 4 and 5:00 they drank some coffee and a small glass of *aguardiente* which was said to be a specific against malaria although they were already taking quinine, a standard protection against that dread disease. Once they got underway at 5:00 the peons paddled steadily until 11:00 when they would stop to eat their midday repast and rest in hammocks. By 3:00, when the hottest part of the day had passed, the party continued on its way for two or three hours more until the peons found a beach suitable for camping overnight. On the fourth day, about two hours' sail from the confluence of the Tua with the Meta River, the travelers

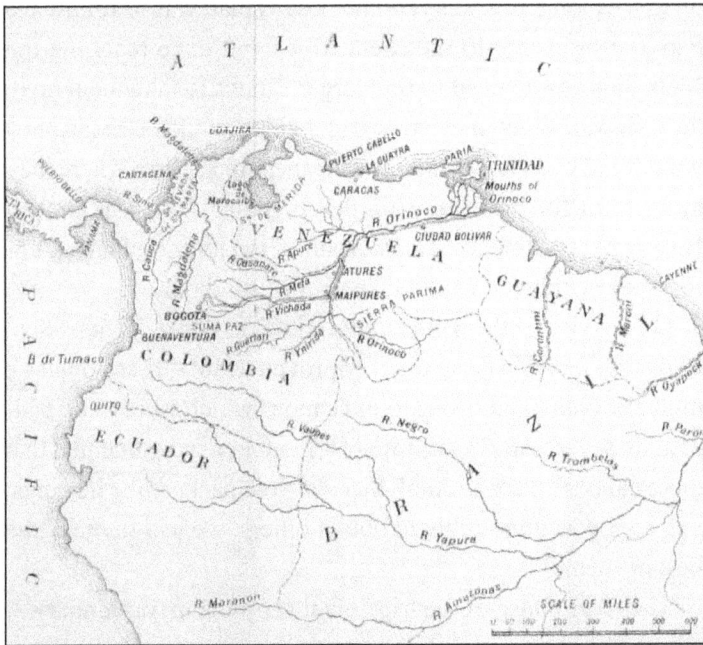

Pérez Triana's route to the Atlantic

stopped at a large cattle ranch called Santa Barbara where the owner provided them with a typical *llanero* dinner: meat roasted over a bonfire, plantains, and coffee.[38]

Continuing on they soon reached the Meta River which being wider and deeper than the Tua enabled them to exchange their small boats for larger canoes. The Meta flowed entirely through Colombian territory as it advanced in large, winding curves eastward towards the Orinoco. Various native tribes inhabited both sides of the river. After four days of navigation, the Pérez party reached the rather large settlement of San Pedro del Arrastradero, which had a population of some 150 inhabitants. At this point they decided to abandon the Meta in favor of taking the Muco River to the Vichada River which offered a more direct passage to the Orinoco.[40] Since some of the peons who had started the trip wished to go no farther, Leal replaced them with natives who were willing to work for a few days at a time in returned for being compensated in kind, i.e., goods such as a handkerchief, a pound of salt, an empty bottle, or a strip of gaudy silk. The group then continued first for six days along the Muco and then along the Vichada: "The navigation of which," as Pérez observed, "proved to be much longer than we had expected."[41]

Without Pérez Triana's knowledge, Leal had told the natives that the party was made up of missionaries, probably in the belief that missionaries were more likely to be welcomed and assisted than any other wayfarers. One day when they stopped at noon, the travelers were surrounded by a "swarm of Indians, males and females of all ages, who came either from the forest or in canoes." The native captain told Leal that mothers had brought their children to be baptized. Unable to dissuade them, Leal told them that Pérez Triana was the chief missionary, but when a native woman discovered that he was not tonsured, she would not accept the lie. Leal took her instead to Alex who being completely bald was accepted by the woman as an authentic man of God. The travelers improvised a christening ceremony that satisfied the natives and "baptized" eight or ten children before the encounter was over.

The next three weeks followed each other in seemingly endless succession creating a sense of monotony and weariness. After 25 days on the Vichada, the group encountered Valente, a Venezuelan manioc trader, who told them that they were still two or three days' journey away from reaching the Orinoco. In due course they arrived at the village of Santa Catalina where they were greeted by Aponte, a Venezuelan who had been appointed as governor of Venezuela's Amazon Territory. Aponte had come to Santa Catalina with the hopes that the natives in that locality might have a cure for the cataracts that covered his eyes. He was accompanied by Figarella, a young Corsican who had a well-stocked medicine chest. Figarella was able to cure one of the members of the Pérez party who had come down with a fever, and he also prepared some excellent meals with turtle eggs, wild-boar meat, and fresh fish.

Two days after leaving Santa Catalina, the travelers reached the Orinoco. At Maipures, where more Venezuelan authorities were stationed, they looked for a pilot to guide them over the rapids which extended five to six miles in length before breaking open into the current of the river. Fortunately they located Gatiño, a man who agreed to help them for 100 dollars if they would wait for him to pack the tonka beans and rubber he had collected.[42] Here, for the first time on their journey, numerous insects assaulted the travelers forcing them to seek protection by using mosquito netting. They also became aware of the mistreatment of the unfed, whip-driven natives, whom the government functionaries methodically plundered and murdered as they forced them to gather rubber and tonka beans without pay.

After three days, Gatiño, accompanied by his wife and four children, returned to Maipures with his own canoe that was deep, heavy, spacious, and comfortable. To get the three canoes (including Gatiño's) across the rapids, the travelers were obliged to empty them completely and carry their cargo on their backs while the boats shot the rapids. It took ten days to cover the distance from the upper to the lower rapids. By this time, the insect menace had disappeared, but as the food supplies brought by the group were depleted, they were forced to depend upon what fish they could catch from the river.

Not far from the Atures rapids, they stopped at Puerto Real where the canoes could be permanently loaded and made ready to follow the river straight to the ocean. At this juncture Leal considered his task at an end. Leaving the group, he returned to Colombia retracing the route it had just completed. Pérez Triana observed: "If the Meta had seemed large and mighty to us, the Orinoco bore the aspect of an inland sea."[43] Trade winds reappeared often forcing the travelers to wait on shore until they dissipated because it was difficult to make any progress against them. Since the breezes, strongest at midday, raised a great quantity of sand, it was impossible to cook, and on one occasion they had to wait for nearly thirty hours before they could continue their journey.

In due time, they reached an unnamed tent village that was pitched on the bank of the Orinoco with some twenty or thirty canoes moored alongside the shore. Seeing among the canoes a small, one-masted schooner, the travelers decided to acquire it and soon closed a deal with the owner. Transferring their belongings into the new craft, they also obtained needed provisions and set sail as soon as possible. The schooner took them to La Urbana, a settlement featuring adobe houses covered with tiles and a small church. Here they abandoned the schooner for a smaller canoe in which they proceeded to Caicara where they expected to find the steamboats that regularly sailed between Ciudad Bolívar and the Apure River. On learning that that it was not certain when a steamboat might arrive there, they continued canoeing down the river, and on April 20 they reached a small village three hours from Ciudad Bolívar. Pressing on, they proceeded directly to Ciudad Bolívar, and they were delighted to discover that it was a real town with houses, hotels, and churches. After spending a week in the city, they boarded a large steamboat that took them to the Puerto España on the British island of Trinidad. Having successfully escaped almost certain imprisonment in Colombia, Pérez Triana triumphantly sailed from Trinidad for Europe, where with no other resources than his varied talents and tireless energy, he was determined to begin a new life.

In summary, during the eleven years between 1883 and 1894, Pérez Triana's endeavors as a commercial agent seem to have brought more failure than success. His involvement in the attempt to scuttle the Núñez regime by supplying war materiel to revolutionaries led by General Gaitán was ill-fated from the start, and he left New York City leaving his creditors in the lurch. His support for the Ferrocarril de Antioquia brought accusations of dishonest practices from which, despite his protestations, he was never completely absolved. His dramatic exodus from his political enemies in Bogotá by travelling over the Eastern Cordillera and through the Llanos was an amazing adventure that he would later record in both English and Spanish, but his three-years residence—first in Medellín and then in Bogotá—was the last substantial time he would spend in Colombia. Between 1894 and 1902 while living in Paris, Madrid, or London, he remained deeply concerned with developments in his homeland but turned his attention firmly to family affairs and developing his literary talents.

3

A New Life in Europe: Family and Literary Achievements, 1894–1907

*"In order to achieve the possible, it is necessary
to attempt again and again the impossible."*
SANTIAGO PÉREZ TRIANA

As noted in the previous chapter, in August 1893, the Conservative government in Colombia fearing a military revolt from its Liberal opponents, forced ex-President Santiago Pérez de Manosalbas, the leader of the Liberal Directorate, to go into exile. He left Colombia to join his daughter Pauline and her husband in Elberfeld, Germany never to return. In 1894 his son reached Europe after his unorthodox escape across the Eastern Cordillera and through the Colombian and Venezuelan Llanos. During the next six years, the two exiles watched from afar while the Liberal Party moved inexorably toward armed revolt against *Regeneración*.

Miguel Antonio Caro, who was elected president after serving as vice president, ended his administration in 1898 on bad terms with congress and arranged a disastrous succession. He deliberately contrived to exclude men of his own party who had demonstrated willingness to compromise with his Liberal critics. His choice for president was the ailing octogenarian, Manuel Antonio Sanclemente and for vice president, José Manuel Marroquín—a seventy-year old with no political experience. Both candidates were ratified in the election of 1898, defeating their Liberal challengers Miguel Samper and Foción Soto. Serving temporarily as chief executive before Sanclemente's arrival in the capital, Vice President Marroquín offered electoral and judicial concessions that might have mollified the Liberal and Conservative dissidents, but Sanclemente withdrew these olive branches after taking possession of the presidency on November 3, 1898. Ill health soon forced him to desert Bogotá for the warmer climate in Anapoima (Cundinamarca), where he continued to exercise his functions, but with the chief executive physically debilitated and the government weakened by fiscal problems, the militant wing of the Liberals began a revolution. Known as the War of the Thousand Days, it endured for three years and touched to a greater or lesser extent every section of the country.[1]

A New Life in Europe

Without any fixed income during this period, Pérez Triana earned his living by relying on his considerable literary talents to collaborate with journals and newspapers in Spain, France, and England. Sometimes he signed these articles with his own name; others he wrote anonymously or under pseudonyms. Although he had written poems earlier in his career, he began producing them more frequently.[2] In 1899 he published a brief set of verses, *El deber de cantar: cantos colombianos*[3] that he dedicated to his father and his brother-in-law, Herr Essen. Antonio José Restrepo, an Antioqueño Liberal, poet and journalist, wrote the preface to this book that at 15 pages was longer than the six poems that followed it. Restrepo provided a brief sketch of Pérez's career pointing out that when he was forced to make his journey down the Orinoco, his myopia bordered on near blindness. He noted that although Santiago was exiled from his country, he was never exiled from its literature and that he continued to engage the pressing questions facing Colombia. "He spoke, reasoned, persuaded, convinced, and subjugated the most hostile opposition" and called on his fellow patriots to continue to fight with ideas against the wrongs created by *Regeneración*.[4]

Of the six poems included in *El deber de cantar*, perhaps "A mi Padre en el Destierro" (To my Father in Exile) is the most interesting since it reveals both Pérez Triana's attitude toward his exile from Colombia as well as his respect for his father. It reads in part:

No temas que yo incline la cabeza:
    Do not fear that I will bow my head:
no es baldón, mi desgracia, que mancilla.
    it is not an affront, my disgrace, that stains.
Quebrarse en pedazos mi altivez,
    With my pride broken in pieces,
No doblo la cerviz ni la rodilla.
    I do not submit or kneel.
La nube de calumnia que me arropa
    The cloud of slander that covers me
ha de pasar como las nubes pasan;
    has to pass as clouds pass;
brota el acero de entre la ígnea copa
    steel springs forth from the igneous brazier
y se templa en las llamas que lo abrasan!
    and it is tempered in the flames that burn it.

And with reference to his father, he wrote:

Tú eres brazo que lucha y voz que canta,
    You are the arm that struggles and the voice that, sings
y guardas á pesar del tiempo fiero,
    and you keep back in spite of the savage times,
rugidos de león en la garganta,
    the roars of the lion from your throat,
intacto el temple de tu invicto acero.
    intact the temper of your invincible steel.
Y cuando se abra para tí la fosa,
    And when the grave is opened for you,
postrero hogar de la materia inquieta
    last resting place of restless matter
tú dejarás la huella luminosa
    you will leave the luminous mark
del mártir, del maestro y del profeta.
    of the martyr, teacher, and prophet.[5]

Santiago's marriage was perhaps the most important event in his personal life. While living in Germany, he had been involved with various women. He penned "A una desconocida," perhaps his most famous poem, sometime in the 1890s, and the poem reveals his longing to find the right person to share his life.[6] Happily he soon fell in love with Gertrude O'Day, the daughter of Daniel O'Day, a wealthy manager from North America who worked for Standard Oil. Gertrude, born in Titusville, Pennsylvania in 1872, was the fourth child of O'Day's large family that eventually consisted of 12 children. In June 1894 at the age of 22, she travelled with three of her sisters to England.[7] Belisario Plata, a Colombian engineer, who later collaborated with Santiago on the *revista Hispania,* states that Gertrude met her future husband as a student in one of the classes he was offering on different subjects in London.[8] The two made an oddly assorted couple. Far from being an Adonis, Santiago, as described by Nieto Caballero, was "short, fat, with the face of a toad, who peered through very thick glasses." Gertrude, 14 years younger than her suitor, was tall, beautiful, and an heir to a very large fortune. Santiago apparently won her love through kindness, and his ability to talk without ceasing on a thousand different topics, spicing the conversation with anecdotes and interesting stories.

Achieving her father's consent to the marriage proved more difficult. Daniel O'Day was immensely rich and uninterested in literature or in any topic that was not related to stock market dividends.[9] When Gertrude first told him of the Santiago's proposal, her father considered the match outrageous. He imagined all Colombians as rude, uncultured people who lived in jungles, and he dismissed Santiago as a "macaco" (monkey). With much tact Gertrude persuaded him to at least grant her suitor a brief interview, promising that afterward she would break off the engagement if he still objected. When they did finally meet, Santiago displayed such an ability to interest the formidable vice president of Standard Oil that little by little Mr. O'Day warmed up to him, and the brief interview stretched into a two-hour conversation. After Pérez Triana had departed, Gertrude asked her father for his impressions. O'Day responded, "He seemed to me so good, that if you do not marry him, I will marry him." Nieto Caballero adds, "That was the power, nearly hypnotic, that Pérez Triana possessed."[10]

After they were married in Paris on March 29, 1896,[11] their union proved to be a happy one. It provided an oasis for Pérez Tirana where he found ease, understanding, and the overwhelming love which he craved. The couple had only one child—a boy, Santiago Pérez Triana, Jr. known as "Sonny" or Santiaguito, who was born on February 4, 1898. Personal information about Gertrude O'Day Pérez Triana is scanty, but Nieto Caballero describes her as larger than her husband with a very beautiful contralto voice that she perfected in classes she took in Paris where she traveled once a week for lessons.[12] In their obituary of Pérez Triana, the editors of *Hispania* praised her as an "enchanting woman" who was his devoted "companion for the rest of his life and who knew as no one else how to access his intelligence and heart." They added that since Gertrude was North American, "The marriage represented the community of ideals of the two continents and also showed how it was possible and beneficial for two people to share mutual intelligence."[13]

At about the same time as his marriage, Pérez Triana developed a friendship with Robert Bontine Cunninghame Graham (Don Roberto)—another person who would have a significant influence in his literary life and career. Don Roberto (1852–1936) was a Scottish politician, writer, journalist and adventurer. Born in London into a wealthy Scottish family, he was educated at Harrow School and in Brussels. In 1870 at age 17, he set out for Argentina, and he worked there and in Uruguay and Paraguay as a cattle rancher and horse dealer for eight years. Learning to speak Spanish as a native, he developed a strong interest in Spanish American culture and history.

Graham returned to Europe in 1883 after his father died having inherited his family's extensive estates in Scotland. His political career began in 1886 and continued sporadically until his death in 1936. Elected to Parliament as a Liberal, by 1888 he had embraced socialism. Graham became the first Socialist member of British Parliament and the first president of the Scottish Labour Party. As Cedric Watts explains in his biography, however, he was much more than a politician: "By 1888 when he was thirty-five, he was a public celebrity, reported, interviewed, and caricatured in newspapers and magazines, a figure hero-worshiped by some, scorned by others; seen as a mixture of eccentric, dandy, maverick, nobleman, cavalier, revolutionary aesthete, firebrand, humanitarian, and cynic....His masterpiece...was himself, in all his vividness and paradoxical variety."[14]

Graham published in 1895 the first of more than 50 books, articles, and sketches that he would write, and during the next ten years, he cultivated friendships with other celebrated authors of the Edwardian era such as Joseph Conrad, W. H. Hudson, Wilfred Scawen Blunt, and Sir William Rothenstein. He met and corresponded with Henry James, Oscar Wilde, Thomas Hardy, H. G. Wells, Martin Hume, and Roger Casement. Although his narrative works did not reach the standard attained by these individuals, he enjoyed notoriety as a major character due to his distinctiveness and his numerous successes in the generically ambiguous territory of the short "sketch" and in autobiographical travel-writing. G. K. Chesterton proclaimed him "The Prince of Preface Writers." He famously declared in his autobiography that while Graham would never be allowed to be Prime Minister, he instead "achieved the adventure of being Cunninghame Graham," which George Bernard Shaw agreed was "an achievement so fantastic that it would never be believed in a romance."[15]

Don Roberto was six years older than Pérez Triana. Being tall, lanky, bold, and impetuous, he cut a far more dramatic figure than the Colombian. Nevertheless, they seem to have become fast friends for they shared many common qualities and interests. As Sanín Cano observed, they believed that friendship was like a religion based on truth, honesty, and loyalty. Both read widely and intently studied the ways of the human heart. Their literary output was similar in that they wrote short narratives designed to develop an idea, an advice, or a determined sentiment. Politically they were united by liberal prin-

Robert Bontine Cunninghame Graham (1852–1936)

cipals, love of equality, democracy, the horror of war, and all kinds of violence.[16] Don Roberto was a frequent visitor when Pérez Triana was in London, and he introduced Santiago to the other major literary figures of the time.

In 1897, Don Roberto received a letter from Joseph Conrad that was to begin the warmest, most enduring, and most productive of all his literary friendships. Later, he encouraged Conrad to write to Pérez Triana as both men were critical of U.S. territorial and economic ambitions in Latin America. Conrad's letters to Don Roberto make clear that his acquaintance with Santiago's career and the latter's objections to the secession of Panama from Colombia had encouraged him to expand the outline of his masterful novel, *Nostromo* "so that instead of being (as originally planned) a relatively limited work about Italian immigrants to South America, it became a general indictment of economic imperialism—and particularly of that of the U.S.A."[17] Moreover, after the publication of *Nostromo* in 1904—a story of revolution, deception, and self-betrayal in Costaguana, a small fictional South American state—it was obvious that Conrad had used Pérez Triana as a model for the character of Don José Avellanos, the idealistic elder statesman in fictional Costaguana.[18] Historian Malcolm Deas, in his essay "Joseph Conrad: *Nostromo* y Colombia," adds that although Conrad treats José Avellanos ironically, "one can detect in the politics of Costaguana-Sulaco echoes of the views of Pérez Triana regarding the politics of Colombia-Panamá: those that rule in the interior do not understand progress and do not know the customs of civilized negotiations: We are a disgrace and a proverb among the world powers."[19]

On August 5, 1900, Santiago Pérez de Manosalbas died in Paris at the age of 70. Although he was buried in that city's Batignolles cemetery, the former president and Liberal leader was not forgotten by his Colombian colleagues. In 1911 Eduardo Nieto Caballero and Abel Camacho organized a pilgrimage to his tomb that included some 200 Colombians then living in Paris. Pérez Triana travelled from London to join them and delivered "an admirable speech filled with emotion and beautiful phrases."[20] He praised his father as a distinguished Colombian, who although humble in birth and modest in his person, irradiated faith in liberty and love of country. The cult to his memory, he declaimed, "will always be a measure of the elements of true national grandeur."[21] More than half a century later on the initiative of President Eduardo Santos, Santiago Pérez de Manosalbas's remains were returned to Colombia and laid to rest with his ancestors in Zipaquirá, Cundinamarca.[22]

Life in Spain

Although his father-in-law was immensely rich, Pérez Triana was determined not to rely on any potential inheritance that O'Day might eventually leave to his daughter. As a result, the household depended on what he could earn by collaborating with English, French, and Spanish newspapers, while Gertrude also accepted small assignments. In 1900, Dr. Rafael Zaldívar, an ex-president of El Salvador, who had corresponded with Santiago in previous years concerning railroads and other enterprises, arrived in Paris. As head of a Salvadoran delegation, he was planning to attend an Ibero-American Congress concerning sociology and economy taking place in Madrid, and he invited Pérez Triana to accompany him as his secretary. Believing that Madrid would offer greater opportunities to exercise his literary talents, Santiago accepted Zaldívar's offer and moved to Madrid with his wife and small son.

The congress took place at the Biblioteca Nacional de España. Eduardo Zuleta, as secretary of the Colombian Legation in Paris, Madrid, and Brussels, was the official Colombian representative, and the meeting was also attended by such prominent intellectuals as: Mexican Justo Sierra; Venezuelan César Zumeta; Chilean Alberto Blest Gana; and Spaniard Carlos Fernández Shaw. Zuleta recalled that when Pérez Triana arrived, he was the same as always: "expressive, smiling and jovial," however, he attended the sessions in silence and occupied his place at the banquets and receptions listening to the eloquent and brilliant expositions of the others without saying a word. When César Zumeta, a companion of Santiago's in New York, read from his recent book, *El continente enfermo* (The Sick Continent), Pérez Triana listened with attention. Zuleta attributed his uncharacteristic silence to the fact that he had come to the congress as Rafael Zaldívar's secretary and did not want to outshine his mentor on this occasion. Nevertheless, he established good contacts with some of the finest minds of the period that would serve him well in the future.[23]

After the conclusion of the congress, the Pérez Tirana family established a home in Madrid. To make ends meet they started a tea house. Gertrude prepared aromatic beverages, and Santiago handled the sales from his office. In addition, Dr. Zaldívar appointed him *Encargado de Negocios* (chargé d'affaires) for the Salvadoran Legation in Madrid. This position was not especially remunerative, but it enabled him to continue participating in important literary circles. Pérez Triana also edited a short-lived weekly magazine, *America,* that attracted some high-quality essays but brought in little revenue. When that enterprise failed, he fell back on writing for important English and American journals—piece work that paid him in pounds and dollars. He was a frequent contributor to the *revista Hispania*, and he was especially proud of a twenty-peseta payment he received for an article published in a Madrid paper.[24]

In addition, between 1902 and 1906 Pérez Triana published three books, two of which included introductory prefaces by friends who were celebrated European authors. The first, *Reminiscencias tudescas*, featured a prologue by the Spanish diplomat, writer, and critic, Juan Valera, who at the time was regarded as one of the most educated men of the era. In his effusive introduction, Valera observed that Pérez Triana had a "complete knowledge of diverse foreign languages and wrote in Spanish with "tact, beauty, elegance, and grace."[25]

The second book was *Down the Orinoco in a Canoe*, published in New York in 1902 with an introduction by Cunninghame Graham. As noted earlier, the first Spanish edition had been published in Paris in 1897. The English version differed in that it included two chapters on Colombian pre-history and geography and another on the geography of the Llanos region in order to orient English readers unfamiliar with Colombia or with South America in general. In his introduction, Graham stated that the account included much information about horsemanship and was a veritable mine of local customs. He continued:

> Few books of travel which I have come across contain less details of the traveler himself....His strength and valor, and his fertility of brain in times of peril, together with his patience...are not obtruded on the bewildered reader as is usual in like cases....What chiefly seems to have appealed to this unusual traveler was the strangeness and beauty of the long reaches on the interminable waterways, the brightness of the moon, the thousand noises of the desert night, the brilliant birds, kaleidoscopic fish, and the enchantment of a world remote from all that a really well-constituted modern mind makes life endurable.[26]

Undoubtedly thanks to the fame of Graham, who had already published several books in English about South America, the English edition of Pérez Triana's book was reviewed in 16 British and four U.S. newspapers. While some critics faulted him for not being more scientific in recording geographic statistics on his journey, their reviews were quite favorable for the most part. Representative was the *Daily Chronicle* of London's assessment on November 3, 1902 that concluded: "The book truly is worth reading in whatever angle it offers, whether as an account of travels in distant lands filled with good things and curious stories, or as a description of virgin territories, or as a revealing product of the soul of an attractive personality filled with *espirit.*"[27] An unsigned review published in the *New York Times* on May 16, 1903 was less enthusiastic, for the writer observed that during his odyssey, Pérez Triana "had no adventures and does not invent any…but what there is in the story is an endless amount of humor, that is served up not in the Saxon way, but in true, graceful Spanish manner." The critic opined: "There is nothing really novel in the description of a semi-tropical river, but the work is certainly remarkable for originality of thought, sharpness, brightness, and the Spanish coloring."[28]

Down the Orinoco in a Canoe was one of several accounts of excursions to Colombia's eastern tropical plains and Amazonian region that took place at the turn of the twentieth century.[29] It established Pérez Triana's credentials as a reliable observer, so it is not surprising that when Miguel Triana (1859–1931), a Colombian engineer and scholar of the Muisca civilization, completed an extensive trip to Nariño and Putumayo regions sponsored by the Reyes government in 1906, he asked Pérez Triana to write an introduction to the account of his experiences published as *Por el sur de Colombia.*[30] Santiago agreed, and in his lengthy "Prólogo," he described Triana as man of solid knowledge and a tireless student of science and literature. Noting that reading *Por el Sur* reminded him of his own experiences traveling through the Llanos, Pérez emphasized the importance of exploring Colombia's southern regions that held incalculable potential for industry and commerce, and he praised Triana for his rigorous scientific descriptions. Considering the volume as literature, Pérez described *Por el Sur* as a "treasure of dreams dreamed and vivid memories."[31]

In 1906 Pérez Triana produced a very different kind of book, *Tales to Sonny* that consisted of six short tales written for children and dedicated to his son.[32] The volume included: "The Stream," "How the Chimp Family came to the City," "The Galleon," "A Party," "The Land of El Dorado," and "Mina and Bili." In the "Preface," Pérez explained that he had related these stories to eight-year-old Santiaguito during their morning walks through Madrid's leafy Retiro Park in the spring and summer of 1905. "To tell him these stories," he wrote, "was a pleasure for me. He enjoyed them more than I could have hoped." The other children who heard them also found them amusing which was "undoubtedly the highest praise."[33] In the belief that his tales would win universal approval from young people, Pérez published them first in English. He then authorized a Spanish translation by Tomás O. Eastman which appeared two years later as *Cuentos a Sonny*. Eastman explained in his preface that although Pérez Triana's language facility was simply marvelous, he found it difficult to translate what he had written in one language into another, and thus he had prevailed upon his colleague to put the stories into Spanish. Eastman accepted the project enthusiastically noting that, while there was a great abundance of children's tales in English, French, and German literature, few were available to Latin American children since authors who wrote in Spanish tended to regard this genre with disdain.[34] In the view of Eduardo Nieto Caballero, *Cuentos a Sonny* was an enchanting children's book. He added that without moralizing, Pérez Triana succeeded in amusing and instructing young people with tales that adults could enjoy as well.[35]

On September 13, 1906 the death of Daniel O'Day at the age of 62 in the French seaside resort of Royan signaled a major change in Pérez Triana's fortunes. O'Day had retired the previous year from active participation in Standard Oil's affairs after ceding his position to his son, Daniel O'Day Jr. who had been especially trained to take over the job. Freed from his managerial duties, the multi-millionaire made several trips abroad, spending much time in Egypt. In May 1906, he sailed to France from New York accompanied by his second wife, Eliza. Although O'Day was known to be in poor health, his death from the "bursting of an artery" was unexpected. Eliza and five of his children including Gertrude Pérez Triana were beside him on the fatal day in Rouen. His body was subsequently brought back to the United States for burial.[36]

O'Day's death obliged Pérez Triana to move his family from Madrid, where he had been highly regarded, and to establish residence in London in order to administer the large inheritance that his father-in-law had left to Gertrude. It was in London that Nieto Caballero first met Pérez in January 1907. He noted that his appearance and demeanor might even have frightened children who saw him without his thick glasses, but once he began to talk, the magic began:

> The cordiality of his welcome, his joy, his caressing voice were a link and invitation to a fiesta. And he spoke, he spoke, he spoke without tiring about a thousand diverse topics, salting the conversation with anecdotes, with intriguing stories, which he

Santiago "Sonny" Pérez Triana

told with a magical grace....He was extraordinarily
amiable, flattering, and witty. He laughed with his
double chin and with his stomach, with his eyes and
his mustache, which shook over his mouth from
which had come this effusion of enthusiasm.[37]

Relieved of pressing financial obligations, Pérez Triana
could now refocus his attention on world affairs from his home
in England, one of the principal commercial and military powers of the world, and his fine house in London located on 45
Avenue Road, Regents Park became a favorite meeting place
for European and Latin American intellectuals who Pérez welcomed with the same conviviality that Nieto Caballero so
vividly described.

4

Political Activities 1899–1909

"Colombia should not enter any agreement with a foreign
country that will put its national sovereignty in jeopardy."
SANTIAGO PÉREZ TRIANA

The decade between 1899 and 1909 marked another turning point in Colombian history for the War of the Thousand Days (1899–1902), the separation of Panama in 1903, and the dictatorship of Rafael Reyes (1904–9) known as the *Quinquenio* laid the economic and political basis for the consolidation of the modern republic. After Pérez Triana's unorthodox escape from Colombia in 1893, the government officially declared him "a detestable man" (*hombre detestable oficialmente)* and refused to let him return until he resolved alleged improprieties in the dispute over construction of the Ferrocarril del Norte. Despite his exile in Europe, Pérez continued to be deeply concerned about events in his homeland.[1] After a brief review of developments in Colombia during this decade, this chapter will focus on his opposition to the *Quinquenio*, his activities regarding the separation of Panama, his support for the Drago Doctrine, and his participation at the Second Hague Convention of 1907.[2]

Colombia: 1899–1909

In 1899, the partisan politics that had been smoldering for a decade in Colombia erupted into the savage War of the Thousand Days that raged for three years costing thousands of lives and untold damage to the nation's economic infrastructure. Quick to take advantage of the national government's weakened power, Panamanian separatists, who had long struggled to establish independence, seized the twin opportunities afforded by the civil war and renewed U.S. interest in the construction of an inter-oceanic canal. On August 10, 1903 the Colombian Senate refused to ratify the U.S.-sponsored Hay-Herrán Treaty that in exchange for Colombia's surrender of its sovereignty over the proposed canal zone would have provided a $40 million payment to the French concessionary company headed by Ferdinand deLesseps and a mere $10 million to Colombia.[3] Suddenly the Panamanian nationalists had a new and powerful ally. With the assistance of President Theodore Roosevelt who ordered the U.S. Navy to prevent any effort by Colombians to regain control over the rebellious province, the nationalists declared Panama's official independence on November 6. On November 18, they signed a treaty with the United States giving the Yankees the right to construct a trans-isthmian canal.

After winning a disputed election in war-torn Colombia, General Rafael Reyes took office as president on August 7, 1904. Reyes announced a program of national restoration which included importing foreign technology, expanding the export sector, improving internal transportation and communication, and promoting industry and mechanized agriculture. To implement these goals, he was prepared to adopt authoritarian measures. When congress showed every intention of blocking action on his stated projects, Reyes took the unprecedented step of dissolving that body on December 13, 1904. In April 1905, he created his own bipartisan but extralegal National Assembly to stamp his presidential decrees with a seal of legitimacy. He extended his term of office from four to six years, and he exiled or imprisoned critics who protested his policies too loudly. Surviving several assassination attempts, Reyes persevered in his dictatorship until an unraveling financial system combined with public outrage over his campaign to win approval of tripartite treaties signed with the United States and Panama forced his resignation. On June 13, 1909 the general sailed for Europe, ending the *Quinquenio*.[4]

Historians have found the five-year *Quinquenio* a difficult period to evaluate. Most agree that Reyes's insistence on representation for minority parties in the government, his curbing of guerrilla activity in the rural areas, and the professionalization of the army and navy were positive accomplishments. Also earning high marks were the completion of several railroads, improved steamships on the Magdalena, and promotion of textile manufacturing and the banana export industry. Historian Charles Bergquist calls Reyes's fiscal reorganization—which involved rationalizing accounting and payment procedures, the setting up of a central bank, and restoring Colombian credit abroad—an "unqualified success," yet he notes that the political costs were high.[5] Important local interests suffered because of the centralization of departmental revenues, while antagonism rose over the dictator's attempts to break down the departments into small political units and to transfer to the central executive control over immigration, foreign investment, and railroad construction. The system of fiscal monopolies gave rise to allegations of graft, and the 1908 recession in Europe and the United States made borrowing abroad, essential to Reyes's plan, more burdensome than ever. Most of all, with the exception of his closest collaborators—

Baldomiro Sanín Cano, José María Quijano Wallis, and Jorge Holguín—the Colombian political elite found Reyes's autocratic methods intolerable. As historians Jesus María Henao and Gerardo Arrubla have written: "If he [Reyes] had thought more and acted less, if he had urged his views more calmly, his administration would have been free from the Caesarism which preoccupied him [and] material progress would have advanced with respect for the rights and personal guarantees of the citizens." Instead, he governed "without scruples, without respect for the constitution that he helped to issue [and] without regard for the law."[6] Nevertheless, as Darío Mesa points out, his regime drew a line between the old and new Colombia.[7]

Opposition to the *Quinquenio*

Santiago Pérez Triana had succeeded in creating a comfortable and rewarding life for himself and his family, first in Madrid and then in London, but he never stopped thinking of Colombia. While understanding the need to restore stability after the horrendous War of the Thousand Days, he was foremost among the critics of Reyes's virtual dictatorship during the *Quinquenio*. He objected to the general's economic policy of funding public works by negotiating foreign loans, and he was furious at the secession of Panama which he regarded as an act of international piracy.

By December 1904 Pérez Triana had reestablished cordial relations with his cousin, Diego Mendoza Pérez whose mother, Teresa was Pérez de Manosalbas's sister. Mendoza earned a law degree at the Universidad Nacional in 1880, and while residing in Tunja, he worked as a lawyer, teacher, and journalist. In 1891, he moved to Bogotá where he maintained close ties with the leaders of Radical liberalism. In 1905, he served as

Colombian ambassador to Washington, but Reyes terminated him in June 1906 after denouncing him as a traitor for having publicized his personal views concerning the negotiations over Panama. Mendoza spent the next four years in exile in the United States and Spain. He published essays on social problems in Colombia, and his correspondence with Pérez Triana reveals their mutual disdain for the *Quinquenio*. For example, on January 6, 1908, Pérez wrote to Mendoza: "If Reyes might disappear for whatever reason—death, illness or exhaustion (this last point I can never imagine)—I do not believe anything better will come along. The degeneration of character is complete [referring to Colombia], and if redemption comes to us, it will be from where we least expect it."[8]

During the previous year, Pérez Triana published *Desde lejos (asuntos colombianos),*[9] a collection of essays in which he expounded his objections to the policies undertaken by Reyes. His "Carta Abierta" (open letter) addressed to President Reyes serves as the prologue to the book. In this letter Pérez expressed his awareness that post-war conditions in Colombia had precipitated the need for strong leadership when he wrote, "Our last war made manifest that we were on the brink of our own extermination and complete destruction....The Nation was like a ship on fire whose crazed crew left it to float without beacon or direction in the seas of history." Although this situation perhaps justified the actions of the political elites in 1904 who, in the first National Assembly, invested Reyes with absolute powers that annulled republican principles for ten years, Pérez Triana was concerned that the president, ruling without the customary checks and balances of the country's constitution, would succumb to a conspiracy of flattery which would keep him from the light of truth.

Writing as a spokesperson for Colombian concerns that had reached him in Europe, he offered a biting critique of Reyes' policies concerning external public credit and the construction of railways. If the situation remained unchanged, he believed that borrowing from abroad would bring not only economic slavery but also endanger national sovereignty.[10]

Although Pérez Triana was at pains to be diplomatic in his critique of Reyes, the latter regarded his book as a direct condemnation, sparked by his government's ratification of a foreign loan in 1905 that became known as the Holguín-Avebury Convention. Earlier in that year, Reyes had dispatched his close political associate, General Jorge Holguín, to London as a fiscal agent to negotiate new loans and restore Colombia's credit abroad. On April 20, 1905, Holguín celebrated an agreement with the Committee of Foreign Holders of Colombian Bonds in London. The loan that he worked out with British banker and Member of Parliament, Lord Avebury (John Lubbock), the Holguín-Avebury Convention, was generous to Colombia's creditors. As Charles Bergquist explains, by securing the accord, Holguín recognized almost the entirety of the principle and interest due on the national debt, rather than seeking to reduce this financial obligation, a strategy commonly adopted and successfully pursued by other Latin American nations during the same period. In this way, he hoped to re-established Colombian credit abroad, to secure an additional foreign loan, and to place the nation in a favorable position to attract foreign capital considered vital to the development of the nation's export economy based on agricultural and minerals.[11] To be specific, Holguín placed the principal of the loan at £2,700,000. Colombia would pay down the £351,000 in interest owed using 15 percent of the income coming from customs.[12] Holguín was elated on arranging this solution, and after the National Assembly approved the convention on July 26, he recounted his emotion at seeing the name of Colombia erased from the blackboard of delinquent debtor nations at the

London Stock Exchange.[13]

Pérez Triana, however, felt that too high a price had been paid to achieve this result. In the 240 pages of *Desde lejos* that followed his "Carta Abierta," he maintained that the restoration of Colombian foreign credit should have been accomplished on terms more favorable to the nation. Conceding the need for railroads, he suggested that construction be focused on only the most important lines rather than attempting to create a network that difficult geography and scant population could not support. In addition, the government should appoint a special negotiator in charge of construction of national public works, and congress should authorize the president to contract foreign debts for a specific sum exclusively destined for the construction of railroads underwritten by government bonds. Above all, the country should not enter into agreement with any foreign firm that would place its sovereignty in jeopardy. When Colombia approved a contract, it should require that the award of vast tracts of public lands that generally formed a part of the arrangement be given to *colonos* (settlers) who either wanted to cultivate the land or to develop a location near a new railroad. A system to give plots of this land to individuals who had worked to build the railroad would be preferable to handing over enormous sections of national territory to companies that would only use them for speculation. Finally, Pérez Triana suggested that soldiers might be used as day laborers for public works—a guarantee of an available work force that would enhance the attractiveness of acquiring a foreign loan.[14]

Reyes made no reply to the "Carta Abierta" and banned the circulation of *Desde lejos* in Colombia, but General Holguín was incensed by Pérez's critique. In response, he wrote *Desde cerca,* a book defending the regime and extolling Reyes' policies as progressive.[15] Writing in 1909, Pérez countered with another book, *Desde lejos y desde cerca (asuntos colom-*

bianos) that was even more polemical—an exchange which prompted Abel Cruz Santos to call the Holguín-Pérez dialogue "one of the most interesting debates in the economic history of Colombia."[16] Although Pérez Triana was not alone in objecting to the Holguín-Avebury Convention, succeeding developments suggest that this policy approved by Reyes was appropriate. During the remainder of the *Quinquenio*, Colombia complied with its obligations to foreign creditors, and foreign capital began once more to flow into the country, most notably in the field of railroad construction, export agriculture, and mining.[17]

In correspondence between 1908 and 1909 with his nephew Jorge Lagos M., Pérez Triana often expressed his contempt for President Reyes. For example, on February 26, 1909 he wrote from his London address: "In the latest newspapers I have seen that our president is traveling by automobile; Unfortunately, there are not many roads that can accommodate this kind of vehicle. I would be pleased if he might prolong his automobile trip; or that he might decide to go to the North Pole, so that the country with his absence, would enjoy true peace, but these are dreams."[18]

Two letters dated March 4 and March 17 repeated the tenor of these comments. In the first, Pérez objected to Reyes taking credit for building roads in Colombia—some of which had existed since colonial times, while others were at least 20 years old. On March 17 he criticized the dictator's efforts to negotiate additional loans and his attempts to get the National Assembly to approve the treaties that had been signed with Panama and the United States. The timing of Pérez' remarks reflected growing opposition to Reyes within Colombia and especially in the National Assembly.[19]

Ortiz observes that Panama's secession from Colombia affected Pérez Triana more deeply perhaps than any other of the men of the times. Until his death he energetically denounced what he regarded as an "act of international piracy."[20] Others also expressed outrage, but Pérez's views, coming as they did from Europe, carried substantial weight. The denunciations he published in the press of both Europe and the Western Hemisphere produced heartburn in Washington political circles. For many years he attacked President Roosevelt who famously claimed, "I took Panama," with reproaches, caustic ironies, and bitter sarcasm. In 1913 when Estanislao Zeballos, the Rector of the University of Buenos Aires, awarded Roosevelt an honorary doctorate, Pérez's indignation reached its height. In an open letter to Zeballos dated November 24, 1913, he denounced the gesture and pointed out that America's youth would regard it as an example of moral degradation.[21]

In the meantime, between 1904 and 1909, Enrique Cortés for Colombia, Carlos Arosemena for Panama, and Elihu Root for the United States were meeting to negotiate agreements to restore relations among the three states. Their deliberations produced on January 9, 1909 a series of treaties that provided for Colombia's recognition of Panamanian independence, Panama's assumption of a portion of Colombia's national debt, trade concessions for Colombian goods in Panama, and the settlement of the Panamanian-Colombian boundary by accepting Colombian claims in most areas and arbitration over the disputed Juradó region (now part of a municipality of the same name in the Department of Chocó.) Panama and the United States ratified the treaties, but the treaties failed to win approval in Colombia where they became a catalyst for uniting adversaries of General Rafael Reyes' pro-U.S. administration.

One of the most outspoken critics was Pérez Triana who used the occasion on May 1, 1909 to compose a "Letter to President Taft in support of international honor." Stating that he was writing on behalf of millions of Colombians, he urged the United States to reject the treaties and outlined his objections to the *de facto* dictatorship of President Reyes.

With regard to the treaties, he maintained that they favored the United States and Panama in two respects: First, they demanded that Colombia relinquish all claims against the United States for its unjust and prejudicial acts in assisting the separation of one of its territories. Second, they stipulated that Colombia must recognize Panama, a former part of its territory, as an independent sovereign nation and that relations between them would be on a basis of international equality.[22]

A third reservation was more serious. Pérez asserted that the Reyes regime was essentially illegal. As such, its ratification of the treaties could only be spurious: the treaties would be null and void, causing all kinds of difficulties in the future. To support these allegations, he pointed out that under Colombia's constitution, Congress, composed of duly elected senators and representatives, had the exclusive right to ratify treaties. After Reyes took power in 1904, however, he closed Congress and replaced it with a National Assembly made up of individuals that he had personally selected. With characteristic sarcasm, Pérez noted that Reyes could appoint to the National Assembly anyone he chose: "for example, the Cuerpo Nacional de Baile (National Ballet); the Asociación Nacional de Acróbatas (National Association of Acrobats), or the Coro Colombiano de Capilla Sixtina (the Colombian Choir of the Sistine Chapel)."[23]

Pérez charged that Reyes had suppressed the most elemental rights of public life including freedom of speech and freedom of the press, and since the personal liberty of citizens depended on his will or caprice, many men had been imprisoned or exiled. He conceded that only Colombians could remedy these domestic abuses, but the question of the legality of the treaties was an international one. Reyes had submitted it to the National Assembly "but even if the assembly was constituted exclusively of angels instead of men, its ratification would be null and without any value." In order not to be complicit in Reyes' fraud, Pérez urged Taft to demand that the treaties be submitted to a congress popularly elected in accordance with Colombia's laws and constitution.[24]

Pérez Triana's letter to President Taft, published simultaneously in Spanish and English, was widely circulated on both sides of the Atlantic. It established him as a brilliant and effective spokesman for the rights of Latin American peoples with regard to U.S. policy. In addition, it undoubtedly contributed to Rafael Reyes' sudden decisions in early June 1909 to allow a congressional election that gave a majority to a newly organized party, the Republican Union, and to leave Colombia for exile in Europe.

Defender of the Drago Doctrine and Participation in The Hague Convention of 1907

Pérez Triana's essays, published in periodicals and journals between 1899 and 1907, ranged beyond commenting on Colombian affairs to dealing with matters of international importance. After 1903, in addition to denouncing U.S. action in Panama, he became an enthusiastic supporter of the Drago Doctrine, and as a delegate to the Second Hague Convention in 1907, he had an ideal stage on which to defend the Drago Doctrine proposal.

Luis María Drago (1859–1921) was an eminent Argentine jurist and minister of foreign affairs in 1902 when three European states (Britain, Germany, and Italy) imposed a naval blockade on Venezuela to enforce financial claims resulting from that country's default on bonds. On December 29, 1902, Drago sent an official note to the heads of American governments stating that "such use of force was contrary to international law, for the collection of loans by military means implies territorial occupation to make them effective, [and] the suppression or subordination of government."[25] Drago based his opinion on a doctrine advanced by fellow Argentine diplomat and legal scholar, Carlos Calvo, who in 1898 had stated that foreigners who held property in Latin American states and had claims against the governments of such states, should apply to the courts within these nations for redress instead of seeking diplomatic intervention. Drago, however, went further than Calvo by adding that economic claims gave no legal right to intervene militarily in another country. This formulation that he defended in two books, *La República Argentina y el caso de Venezuela* (1903) and *Cobro coercitivo de deudas públicas* (1906), became known as the Drago Doctrine. In a nutshell, it simply stated that although a nation is legally bound to pay its debts, it cannot be forced to do so.[26]

The doctrine was innovative because it categorically rejected the right of military intervention or occupation of a country for the purpose of collecting debts at a time when European powers as well as the United States were carving out empires around the globe. It had overwhelming support from Latin American leaders, but Europeans were unwilling to accept a principle of international law that would limit their right to recover money invested abroad. In December 1904 President Theodore Roosevelt, in a drastic departure from Drago's argument, announced that the United States would intervene directly in conflicts between European and Latin American countries to enforce legitimate claims, rather than having the Europeans press their demands militarily. In keeping with the Monroe Doctrine, he maintained that the United States was justified in exercising "international police power" to put an end to chronic unrest or wrongdoing in the Western Hemisphere. While the original Monroe Doctrine had sought only to prevent European intervention, for the next three decades the U.S. government would use Roosevelt's "Corollary" to legitimize U.S. intervention throughout the hemisphere. Given this state of affairs, and in an effort to defend their sovereignty from outside aggression, it is not surprising that Latin American countries would attempt to get Drago's Doctrine accepted as an international law at the next international conference, the Second Hague Conference of 1907.[27]

Western Hemisphere states were conspicuously absent from the first Hague Conference which met in 1899 after being proposed by Russian Tsar Nicholas II. That event brought together representatives of 26 major world powers who reviewed existing international agreements regarding the laws and customs of land and sea warfare and discussed how peace might be maintained by approving pacts limiting the expansion of armed forces and reducing deployment of new armaments. Of the 26 nations present, only two American nations participated: the United States and Mexico. Although this conference failed to achieve its primary objective, i.e., a limitation on armaments, it did adopt conventions defining the conditions of a state of belligerency and other regulations relating to war on land and sea. Declarations accepted included prohibiting the use of asphyxiating gases, the use of expanding bullets, and the discharge of explosives from balloons. The delegates also created a Permanent Court of Arbitration to deal peacefully with international disputes.[28]

In 1904 U.S. President Theodore Roosevelt proposed the Second Hague Conference that was officially convened in the Dutch Republic by Tsar Nicholas II on June 15, 1907. In attendance were representatives of 44 states including 19 from Latin America thanks to insistence by Russia's embassy in the United States that Hispanic American countries participate in the deliberations. Colombia was among those that accepted an invitation, and its delegation consisted of General Jorge Holguín, General Marceliano Vargas, and Santiago Pérez Triana. Given the latter's well known opposition to Reyes and the *Quinquenio*, his selection for this post is surprising, but Ortiz suggests that his appointment was in recognition of the prestige he enjoyed due to his writings in international journals and his fluency in the various languages that would be spoken at the meeting.[29]

The conference met at The Hague from June 15 to October 18. Again it failed to adopt a proposal to limit armaments. The delegates did, however, approve several conventions relating to: the rights and duties of neutral powers and persons in war on land and sea; the laying of automatic submarine contact mines; the status of enemy merchant ships; bombardment by naval forces in wartime; and the establishment of an international court for arbitration.

For Latin American delegates, the most important debate concerned the employment of force for the recovery of contract debts. Addressing the delegates on July 18, Dr. Drago, as a member of the Argentine Delegation, once again put forward his so-called doctrine: No foreign power, including the United States, could use force against another state to collect debt. The Latin Americans were in complete agreement with this principle, but the U.S. delegation objected, and one of its members, General Horace Porter, was ready with an alternative. In what became known as the Porter Convention, the general suggested that when a country defaulted on its debt, it must submit to a court of arbitration to gain a resolution of how much money was owed and how it was to be paid. If the debtor state refused to accept an offer of arbitration or if it accepted the offer but prevented any compromise being reached, or if, after an arbitration hearing, it refused to carry out the decision, the creditor state could then resort to military action to force payment.[30]

Latin Americans were adamantly opposed to Porter's alternative, and on July 23, Pérez Triana rose to articulate their objections. Making clear that his country, Colombia, had well-established credit, he went on to confirm that the collection of public debts was of major interest to the Latin America countries. Their great natural wealth would doubtlessly require capital from abroad for its exploitation, but the principle of forced collections of loans could only be applied when the debtor was weak and the creditor was strong. He conceded that in spite of all prudence, a government might be unable to meet its pecuniary obligations due to internal revolutions, natural disasters, or sustained low prices in the sale of national products, but the problem with arbitration was that the debtor state might fail to comply, not from lack of will, but from lack of being able to pay. A ruling by an arbitration court would not change the situation of the debtor state nor augment its resources, and if military coercion was employed, the debtor country would have to resist and lose its sons in a defensive war. Such a method of debt collection was counter-productive and clearly no longer acceptable, since most civilized countries had already suppressed laws requiring debtors to go to prison. "The conclusion is monstrous," Pérez Triana thundered. "The insolvent debtor is set free, but the insolvent nation faces war." He continued:

> We proclaim the inviolability of the sovereignty of States in accordance with the Drago Doctrine... .We reject the use of force. If you ask what is to be done, I reply: If you cannot resolve the problem satisfactorily and with justice, let things take their course. Nations are not immortal. That is to say: national debts are not absolute, and what one generation doesn't pay, the following generation will. It

would not be a miracle, but a grave error to leave
in the hands of the financiers, among which there
are some who are not angels, the means to facilitate
imperialist wars more or less masked in their ten-
dencies against weak nations.[31]

Pérez Triana's speech proved a "true revelation" for the
other delegates who were accustomed to hearing orations in
barely understandable French (the language of the conference).
His pure, eloquent French captured their admiration and won
great applause. French statesman, M. Léon Bourgois, the English lord, Sir Ernest Mason Satow, and the German Baron,
Marschall de Bieberstein each congratulated him, and with
characteristic flourish, Pérez Triana greeted Bieberstein in German.[32] In recognition of his oratorical skills, the delegates, by
unanimous consent, voted that Pérez Triana should make the
final speech closing the conference.

Despite Pérez's personal triumph, it must be underscored
that the delegates never actually discussed the pros and cons
of Drago's Doctrine. Instead, they accepted the Porter Convention put forth by the U.S. delegation. In other words, they
adopted an international convention prohibiting recourse to
armed force for the recovery of contract debts claimed from
the government of one state by another government on behalf
of its nationals but with the proviso that armed force could still
be used if the debtor state refused to accept an offer of arbitration; if it accepted the offer but prevented any compromise
being reached; or if, after an arbitration ruling, it refused to
carry out the decision.[33] Between 1909 and 1911, 17 states including Mexico, Nicaragua, Haiti, Guatemala, and Panama ratified this convention. The remaining Hispanic American
states—Argentina, Bolivia, Colombia, Dominican Republic,
Ecuador, Peru, Salvador, and Uruguay—signed but with reser-

vation.[34] On signing the pact the Colombian delegation made clear that it would not accept the use of force for the collection of debts of whatever nature, and that it would only accept arbitration after the definite decision of the tribunals of the debtor countries.[35]

Pérez Triana's fiery presentations in French and English won praise from journalists in Europe and America. For example, the *Courrier de la conférence* in its review of the discussion of the Drago doctrine on July 19, cited the support for its acceptance offered by "Sr. Triana in his eloquent and convincing speech."[36] The London *Tribune* on the same day noted that Pérez Triana's speech, "typically short and caustic, filled with sarcasm and grand truths, and delivered with the force and passion of the genuine orator" had made him "one of the most notable people at the Conference."[37]

At the end of the conference, Pérez Triana returned to London as an individual of world stature, for as W. T. Stead proclaimed: "With that formidable orator had appeared a new continent."[38] It was for his participation at The Hague Conference that the modern Colombian journal *Credential Historia* in its series "Personajes del Año" selected Pérez Triana as "Man or the Year" for 1907 explaining: "Santiago Pérez Triana in impeccable English pronounced a rousing speech in support of the thesis of the Argentine Drago. The speech, that provoked opposite reactions in favor and against, praised in London and attacked in Bogotá, elevated the figure of Pérez Triana into the international forefront for some months. Sufficient merit to be considered the most outstanding Colombian of 1907."[39]

Pérez Triana continued to advocate the adoption of the Drago Doctrine as an international law for the rest of his life. In 1908, he wrote an "Advertencia Preliminar" (Preliminary Warning) to a volume entitled *La Doctrina Drago: colección de documentos* published by Wertheimer, Lea & Company of

London that included: an introduction by William T. Stead; Spanish translations of all speeches presented at the 1907 Hague Conference; and 19 accounts of the meeting reported in European and U.S. journals. Pérez began the "Advertencia" by pointing out that the very fact that Latin American countries were invited to attend The Hague conference was a "kind of definite recognition of their sovereignty and that they were no long colonies of Spain and Portugal. Throughout history powerful states have abused weaker states. Now these nations have a voice."[40] He then reviewed the activities of the First Hague Conference in 1899 and the subsequent international events that led up to Luis María Drago announcing his doctrine in 1902.

He explained again why the Drago Doctrine was so important for Latin American nations. Because these countries had such vast territories, he noted, they had relied on foreign capital to exploit their potential assets. A constant state of political turmoil throughout the nineteenth century had often made it impossible for them to repay their debts, but certainly capitalists who invested money had been aware of their precarious financial condition. In the future, Latin American countries would continue to solicit and obtain loans from Europe, and it was quite possible that they might not be able to meet their commitments. The Doctrine proclaimed by Dr. Drago would protect their sovereignty as well as the interests of universal peace.[41]

The proposition offered by the U.S. delegation and adopted by the Conference, Pérez continued, was a step forward toward justice by agreeing that armed force may not be used in the collection of contractual debts except as a last resort. Nevertheless, it fell short of the Drago Doctrine in that it permitted attacks on the sovereignty of states that failed to accept arbitration or which after arbitration failed to carry out the agreement. The Latin American delegates, in accepting the North American alternative with provisos, did so in the sense that half a loaf was better than none, but the Drago Doctrine, "even though it was not specifically studied and discussed in the Second Peace Conference, was the only new and fertile principle submitted for the consideration of the delegates of those nations in that assembly."[42]

In the final section of "Advertencia Preliminar," Pérez brought up another issue that reflected his continued opposition to Reyes' *Quinquenio*. He pointed out that the real threat to the sovereignty of a nation came not from the outside but from its own people, i.e., presidents who by their acts undertake obligations outside the power of the country, who governed by their own convenience, annul individual rights, mute the popular voice, and establish cruel regimes in the name of democratic republics.[43] Such individuals could become wealthy by obtaining loans from foreign countries, which, if they were overthrown, they could use to go into exile. In this sense, the Drago Doctrine that protected sovereignty would also protect leaders who have taken over a country. This potential threat did not invalidate the Doctrine, but Pérez concluded that until Latin American nations had quelled their political disturbances, it would be difficult to achieve universal acceptance of any doctrine endorsing their absolute sovereignty.[44]

In a recent article published in *Diplomatic History*, Juan Pablo Scarfi points out that "Drago never conceived his doctrine as an international law principle," yet by promoting the Porter Convention as an alternative, Elihu Root and James Brown Scott, the U.S. delegates at The Hague Conference of 1907, were co-opting its essence into the ideology of the Monroe Doctrine.[45] In spite of their efforts, Scarfi argues that the Drago Doctrine was "a pioneering initiative to Pan-Americanize the [U.S.] doctrine" and thus contributed to an ongoing effort by Latin American international lawyers and politicians to create by 1930 the institutionalization of the Monroe Doctrine

as a multilateral and Pan-American principle of non-interven-
tion.[46] Pérez Triana's promotion of Drago's formula was
clearly an important factor in this process.

Between 1899 and 1909, Pérez remained in close touch with
events in his homeland. As a delegate to The Hague Conference in 1907 and in his support of the Drago Doctrine, he
emerged as one of the most celebrated supporters of Latin
American rights vis-à-vis the United States. He expressed his
opposition to the *Quinquenio* in his publications and in his letters to his cousin, Diego Mendoza. On September 9, 1908 he
wrote to the latter that he believed the time had come to over-
throw Reyes by military means, and on February 20, he con-
fessed that he was at work on a book accusing the clergy of
supporting the regime.[47] On May 19, however, he wrote to
Mendoza that he had received news from Bogotá and Medellín
that "Reyes is fallen!" and that for the time being he was aban-
doning work on his book in order to see how events would
play out in Colombia.[48]

"Our Man in London:"
Minister Plenipotentiary, Editor,
and Diplomat, 1909–1916

"We must fortify the inviolability of the continent
for the pressing hour gives no quarter, and the omission of
today may be the irreparable calamity of tomorrow."

SANTIAGO PÉREZ TRIANA

After the fall of Reyes in 1909, the Republican Union party took power in Colombia, and Pérez Triana made peace with the new leaders. During the last seven years of his life, afflicted by failing sight and poor health, he served as Colombia's minister plenipotentiary to London, editor of his journal *Hispania,* and delegate to the First Pan-American Financial Conference, which took place in Washington, D.C. in May 1915. With the Great War raging in Europe and despite his youthful affection for Germany, he strongly supported the allied cause at the conference. The object of this chapter is to trace these developments which would crown his long and varied career.

A New Regime in Colombia

A few days before June 13, 1909, when Rafael Reyes startled Colombians by abruptly going into exile, the dictator presided over a congressional election that gave a majority to a newly organized party, the Republican Union. Led by Liberals and Historical Conservatives, the party was committed to a program of strict republicanism, bipartisan participation in government, and laissez-faire economics. Its members dominated the National Assembly that was installed on July 20. After electing General Ramón González Valencia to complete Reyes's term of office, extended to August 7, 1910, they proceeded to dismantle most of the repressive measures of the *Quinquenio*. Within a few months they approved laws that reduced the presidential term to four years, prohibited immediate reelection, provided for annual meetings of Congress, restored direct presidential election, and made provisions for minority representation. Yet the Reyes legacy remained intact in other ways. Political stability replaced the ideological contentiousness, partisan exclusiveness, chronic civil war, and ephemeral constitutions that had characterized the decades before the dictator. The new leaders continued his policy of promoting export growth and selective protectionism for domestic industry while repudiating measures that might threaten the interest of the large landowners.[1]

The National Assembly elected Carlos E. Restrepo, an Antioqueñan Conservative and leader of the Republican Union, as president for the period from 1910 to 1914. Restrepo was succeeded by another Conservative, José Vicente Concha (1914–18). As Liberals struggled to regroup after their catastrophic defeat in the War of the Thousand Days, Conservatives continued to dominate the national government until 1930.

Many of these administrations were bipartisan in composition, and the principle of minority representation assured both traditional parties membership in the national legislature. Pérez Triana had full confidence in the new leaders, and in 1909 he accepted General González Valencia's appointment to serve as Envoy Extraordinary and Minister Plenipotentiary of Colombia to Great Britain, a post he continued to hold after the election of President Restrepo.[2] In the Congress of 1909 and the National Assembly of 1910, Pérez Triana was elected in absentee by people in the city of Manizales. As Minister to Great Britain, he could gracefully decline serving as a representative of Manizales by stating that his new duties would not allow him to leave London.[3] His cousin Diego Mendoza Pérez, however, returned to Colombia in 1910 after the new government absolved him of being a "traitor" for having publicized his personal views concerning the negotiations over Panama while serving as Colombian ambassador to the United States.[4]

Envoy Extraordinary and Minister Plenipotentiary

The immediate problem Pérez Triana faced in his diplomatic capacity arose at the beginning of December 1909 when the London dailies published a cable from Bogotá signed by an English person who claimed to be acting for other Englishmen. The cable reported that the Colombian Minister of Hacienda y Tesoro, Simon Bossa, had declared that the government would not pay the interest on its external debt. The *Quinquenio*, Bossa explained, had exhausted the national treasury, and he could no longer fulfill the promised payments Reyes had contracted. This announcement produced great alarm among holders of various Colombian debts listed on the London stock market that had been guaranteed by the Colombian government. The Holguín-Avebury Convention, bitterly opposed by Pérez in 1907, had encouraged these loans. They had produced an estimated $4 million, but after the ouster of Reyes, repayment of these debts came due. Facing this crisis, Pérez Triana cabled Bogotá for instructions.

The government replied by authorizing him to dispute the English claim, and it dispatched José Vicente Concha to London to work with him to resolve the crisis. The two men fashioned a deal whereby the government was able to obtain a loan of £28,000 to pay off the coupons of debt consolidated in conformity with the Holguín-Avebury arrangement. The drawback was that the London bankers demanded that Colombia pledge ten times the value of the loan. Left with no other options, they agreed to these conditions, and by January 1, 1910 the new loan had restored the credit of the Republic.[5]

Colombia's need for foreign investment remained an ongoing problem during the Republican Era, and Pérez Triana immediately began negotiations for another loan to pay off obligations incurred by interest on the mortgage of the Ferrocarril de Giradot and an entity called the Colombian National Railway Company. By March 1910 following the instructions of the government, he and Concha obtained and submitted a proposal to the government for a loan of £500,000 underwritten by London bankers. Despite the support of President González Valencia, the National Assembly refused to ratify the new agreement, but after Carlos Restrepo assumed the presidency the following August, the new congress approved the loan.[6]

For the next year, Pérez Triana dedicated himself to dealing with problems of the national economy and the development of commercial interchange. The publication of his *Eslabones sueltos (asuntos colombianos)* (*Loose Ends*) at the end of 1910 provides a record of his activities and documents his efforts to find lessees for the Muzo emerald mines (which he saw as the nation's most pressing need) and to resolve the debts that had been incurred to underwrite the Ferrocarril de Giradot.[7] As historian James Henderson points out, Pérez Triana gave his argument in favor of seeking foreign loans an honorable cast by tracing "popular misery [and] the many evils afflicting Colombia" to a lack of personal capital. "Without [money]," he lectured, "moral progress is impossible."[8] Henderson adds that modern studies confirm Pérez's perception that Colombians had very little disposable capital, and the scarcity of investment capital made it increasingly necessary that, however distasteful, the country improve its relations with the United States and settle the dispute over the recognition of Panamanian independence.[9]

Near the end of 1911, Pérez Triana received from Bogotá a plan dated October 16, 1911 for unifying Colombian debts prepared by a New York banker, Alfred Meyer, and his Colombian collaborators. After studying the proposed arrangement, Pérez informed President Restrepo that he regarded it as detrimental to Colombia's interests. Despite his objections, Restrepo's Minister of Hacienda, Francisco Restrepo Plata, and his undersecretary of the treasury, Ricardo Hinestrosa Daza, signed the contract on January 20, 1912. Pérez stated that if the European parties accepted the contract, Restrepo Plata and Hinestrosa Daza would have to convince Congress to approve it despite their total lack of understanding of the country's financial affairs. Since his objections in this matter had not been taken into account he felt he could no longer serve as Colombia's minister plenipotentiary to England or as head of the legation to Madrid. In a letter to President Restrepo dated July 31, 1912, he announced his resignation of both posts which Restrepo accepted. He then went on to publish a pamphlet, *Unificación de deudas (asuntos colombianos)* (*Unification of Debts*) expounding upon his objections to the contract.[10]

Soon afterwards Pérez Triana suffered a severe stroke that left him near death. His doctors attributed it to overwork and recommended complete rest. After three months of recuperation, Pérez resumed his normal lifestyle as editor, writer, host, and gourmet, but he suffered from partial paralysis for the rest of his life.[11] Despite his health problems he did not abandon all official diplomatic activity: as late as 1916 he was representing the Republic of Nicaragua as Envoy Extraordinary and Minister Plenipotentiary to England.[12]

Revista *Hispania*

Since he was no longer officially representing Colombia in London, Pérez dedicated his activities to building a new journal designed to be an outlet for the opinions, concerns, and defense of people who spoke Spanish. His broad contacts with public financiers and politicians enabled him to amass the funding needed to begin the enterprise that had been a lifetime goal. *Hispania,* the name of his first short-lived journal in Madrid, was also the name of the new publication in London. Pérez established an office at 7 Sicilian Avenue, Southampton Row, and here he edited the new journal. The first issue appeared on January 1, 1912. Monthly issues continued until June 1916 so that before its demise *Hispania* achieved a total output of 54 issues in five volumes.

Pérez was fortunate that there were several Colombians living in London at that time who were eager to collaborate. Especially helpful was Antioqueño essayist and educator Baldomiro Sanín Cano, a supporter of Reyes, who had been sent by him to London in 1909. After Reyes left Colombia, Sanín Cano stayed on in London offering classes, translating works, and studying in the British Museum. A good friend of Pérez Triana since 1893, he served as co-editor of the new

journal. Other colleagues included: José María Núñez Uri-
coechea, who was knowledgeable about financial matters; Saturnino Restrepo, an astute critic, writer and secretary of the
Colombian Legation; Tomás O. Eastman, who shared with
Pérez the goal of educating people; and Enrique Pérez Lleras,
a former Liberal deputy from Barranquilla whose experience
as an editor and journalist in Bogotá enabled him to assist in
resolving the problems involved with running a journal.
Colombians residing in Paris also contributed as well as some
Spaniards such as Luis Araquistain Quevedo and Faustino Bal-
lvé who lived in London, and Miguel Unamuno, Ramón Pérez
de Ayala, and José Sánchez Rojas, who wrote from Spain.
Other writers whose essays appeared in the journal included
Robert Bontine Cunninghame Graham, James Fitzmaurice-
Kelly, and Gabriel Zéndegui, secretary of the Cuban legation
in London.[13]

In the January 1, 1912 inaugural issue, Pérez Triana declared his editorial objective:

> *Hispania* wants to carry to people who speak Span-
> ish some *aliento* (breath, inspiration) that will
> awaken their lives....We will all win if we know
> what our people are saying. I should like *Hispania,*
> also—within the reduced range of its forces—to
> bring to Spanish peoples and to others a message
> that is worthy of them, that illuminates minds or
> moves consciences. As the gold standard in com-
> mercial exchanges, *Hispania* should like to help es-
> tablish the golden discernment of serene logic and
> of common sense in the life of our peoples.[14]

In accordance with these goals, the 28 pages of each
monthly issue of *Hispania* contained articles dealing with

economy, sociology, and the rights of nations—topics then being debated in parliaments, political circles, and other publications. The editorial notes and in-depth articles that Pérez Triana wrote for each issue, signed with his own name and the pseudonyms "Hispano" or "A. de Manos Albas" according to the importance of the document, had the virtue of awakening a new awareness of the problems of international relations. "He takes upon himself," wrote one reviewer, "the defense of weak peoples and appears before the concourse of nations as a herald of peace and justice."[15]

Pérez Triana's articles in *Hispania* were not limited to political commentary. For example, in March 1912 he marked the centenary of Charles Dickens's birth with an essay extolling his place in English literature as second only to Shakespeare and emphasizing the universality of his books.[16] On May 1, 1912 *Hispania* reported the sinking of the *Titanic*—a personal tragedy for Pérez since among the passengers who were lost was his good friend, William T. Stead, a man who he described as being like "all reformers and apostles and propagandists, a believer and not a skeptic; better armed with confidence than with precaution and more with enthusiasm than shrewdness."[17] Pérez also wrote for the journal *Cuadros de costumbre (Descriptions of Local Culture)* based on his memories of Colombia. One of the best known was "De la vera del camino" (By the roadside) which contained three short pieces, "Piedras de moler" (Millstones), "El Sombrero" (the Hat), and "Sillas de montar (Saddles)."[18]

These and similar essays enhanced the broad cultural appeal of *Hispania,* but without doubt it was the sovereignty of Spanish American peoples that most preoccupied its editor and the cause to which he dedicated gigantic effort. U.S. complicity in Colombia's loss of Panama and its imperialistic policies in Central America and the Caribbean provided him with the rationale to urge all the nations who had freed themselves from Spain to join together into a force that could protect their future destinies.

At around this time Pérez Triana, like many other contemporary writers, was intrigued by arguments presented by Norman Angell in a book first published in the United Kingdom in 1909 under the title *Europe's Optical Illusion* and republished the following year as *The Great Illusion*.[19] In these volumes, Angell maintained that the economic interdependence of the countries of Western Europe had rendered war between them impossible. If a conquering power confiscated property in the territory it seized, "the local population's incentive to produce would be sapped, rendering the conquered area worthless. Thus the conquerors would have to leave property in the hands of the local population while incurring the costs of conquest and occupation."[20] Pointing out that military confrontation was economically harmful to all those involved, Angell concluded that the belief that nations could gain anything by war was simply a "great illusion."[21]

Pérez Triana could hardly ignore a book so often reprinted and widely discussed throughout Europe. He wrote his most coherent critique of Angell's argument in his introduction to Saturnino Restrepo's Spanish translation of *The Great Illusion* (*La Grande Ilusión*) published in Paris in 1913.[22] In presenting the book to a Spanish-speaking audience, Pérez stressed that Angell described the most powerful nations of Europe as separated into two "distinct groups" that were potentially antagonistic and hostile to one another: England, France and Russia on one side, and on the other, Germany, Austria, and Italy, with the rest of the European states serving as satellites. Because each group was building up its military capabilities, Angell argued that these preparations would help to maintain peace, but Pérez pointed out that the cost of their military budgets weighed heavily on the proletarian masses which in time might provoke internal rebellions. Despite a plethora of popular misgivings, both groups continued to increase their armies, ships, and fortifications, and two international meetings called to limit the arms race had failed to find a solution.

Pérez observed that Angell had not considered that peace in Europe did not rule out the possibility of imperialistic wars to conquer territory, and remarked that if barbarism (i.e., imperialism) were enthroned in Europe, it "would be impossible for the rest of the world to avoid its deleterious influences."[23] Spanish-speaking people, Pérez Triana advised, should study Angell's book from a different point of view depending on which side of the Atlantic they were located. For Spain there was undoubtedly a real threat, but in America thanks to the Monroe Doctrine, an imperialistic invasion from Europe was unlikely. Nevertheless, Iberian America knew by painful experience that armies could be converted into elements of tyranny. Increasing military budgets could easily lead to exalted patriotism and suffering of the masses. Pérez concluded that one could only hope that Angell's argument i.e., that confrontations between European powers would inevitably lead to economic destruction making war unlikely—would hold equally true in the Western Hemisphere.[24]

The "Introducción" was actually the third time that Pérez Triana addressed Angell's theories, for he had previously developed his response at greater length in two essays in 1912. He published the first one, "Memorandum Sent to the Latin-American Governments" in *Hispania* on March 1 and the second, "A Manifest to the Peoples of America: Wanted: a Revised and Extended Monroe Doctrine," in the March 1912 issue of *The Review of Reviews*.[25] In the "Memorandum" he noted that the two alliances of the Great Powers of Europe had been successful in maintaining peace on that continent, but that they had not brought peace to the rest of the world. At the same time, a relentless wave of European acquisition of territory in foreign lands had occurred, entailing violence, bloodshed, and devastation. To maintain domestic peace, the European powers had found it necessary to create large land and naval forces that in turn brought about a constant increase of taxation on the masses. They had adopted territorial expansion as a way to control an overflow of population and used it as a safety valve for avoiding potential domestic revolts, since large numbers of people from the mother countries could immigrate to the newly conquered territories. But this strategy, however expedient for Europe, did not take into account the objections of the occupants of annexed territories—"a most amazing moral incongruity."[26]

According to Pérez Triana, the essential condition for a given territory to be suitable for the purposes of expansion was that it had to be in weak hands, and since the distribution of available territory in the Old World was practically complete, it had become indispensable for Europe to find new fields of action. The Americas had thus far enjoyed immunity from European political expansion, but conditions in the Latin part of the continent were essentially those of weakness arising from the disparity between the size of the population of each republic and its respective territorial responsibility. President James Monroe's timely declaration in 1823 had closed the American continents to European conquest for all time, but his doctrine had not stopped the North Americans themselves from seizing territory belonging to other nations. To restore hemispheric trust, Pérez Triana suggested that "the United States and the other Republics of America solemnly declare that conquest is forever proscribed from the continent of Americas, and let them pledge themselves not to practice or to tolerate the conquest of territory."[27] In closing his memorandum, he cited the words of President Taft who was seemingly renouncing further U.S. aggression, when he proposed in January 1911 that matters of national honor and other questions of difference should be referred to a court of arbitration.[28]

Two months later Pérez Triana expanded these points in his "Manifest to the People of America: Wanted: A Revised and Extended Monroe Doctrine." This essay was divided into two parts, "The Menace of Expansion" and "How to Protect the New World" and was published in the March 1, 1912 issue of *Hispania* and reprinted by William T. Stead in the March issue of *The Review of Reviews*.[29] Stead introduced the piece (signed by Pérez with his pseudonym A. de Manos Albas) as a "masterly presentation of a plea for taking a forward step towards the world's peace…written by one of the shrewdest and ablest public men to whom Latin America has given birth in our time."[30]

In "Menace of Expansion," Pérez underscored the difference between the theory of international law, which was "the highest ideal, embracing liberty and charity, for where oppression or cruelty exists, justice ends," and the practice of international law, "which embraces violence, bloodshed, rapacity, mendacity, and hypocrisy." Although no war had occurred in Central Europe during the last 40 years, peace in Europe did not bring peace to the rest of the world. Instead, "the tide of European expansion, which has always meant violence, had submerged every available spot on the continents and the islands throughout the Old World."[31]

Pérez was especially incensed by Italy's declaration of war on Turkey and its invasion of Tripoli on September 29, 1911—decisions that fulfilled its long-desired goal of establishing a colony in North Africa. "One is prepared for anything from Russia," he declared, but the action of the Italian government was an unexpected shock. "Never in the history of that glorious land...was there such ruthless iniquity, in conception and in performance, as in the Tripoli expedition."[32] Although each of the two opposing groups in Europe contained reactionary and enlightened nations, no hope could be placed on the latter to ameliorate the policy of their allies. Unlimited armaments had become a necessity, and their cost was constantly on the increase. If millions of trained soldiers returned to civilian life, the hour for radical and even violent changes was certainly within measurable distance, and the expansion of the armed forces was considered an offset against such menaces.[33]

In "How to Protect the New World" Pérez Triana explained that the Western Hemisphere had remained immune from Europe's renewed imperialism thanks to the Monroe Doctrine. Since winning independence the Americas had received a steady stream of European immigrants, for the attraction of the New World to the European masses was as irresistible as the tides of the ocean. The process of developing and strengthening the American nations with European wealth and immigrants was bound to continue unless some fundamental transformation of existing conditions arose. Despite population growth, immense territory remained available for European expansion—open territory that offered many more amenities than the lands of Africa and made the condition of the American nations one of weakness. As a result, Pérez argued, "No effort should be spared to strengthen a protection which has proved so efficacious and decisive in the past."[34]

Latin American immunity from European aggression was due to President Monroe's declaration, but immunity from conquest was not absolute because the North Americans themselves had on occasions turned into conquerors. If the U.S. government should declare "that the era of conquest of territory on the American continent has been closed to all and forever, beginning with themselves, the brooding storm of distrust would disappear from the Latin-American mind."[35] Pérez Triana concluded the "Manifest" by suggesting that President Taft had a unique opportunity to amend the Monroe Doctrine as previously explained since encouraging cordial cooperation between Latin America and the United States was as important in his day as it was in the time of President Monroe: "The exclusion of conquest of territory as a fundamental principle of international life on the American continent should be solemnly proclaimed by all the American nations; they should all pledge themselves to maintain it. The sands are running in the glass of Time; tomorrow it may be too late."[36]

In his "Memorandum to the Latin American Governments" and his "Manifest to the Peoples of America" Pérez Triana made a compelling argument for the Pan-Americanization of the Monroe Doctrine, an argument which also formed part of his refutation of Angell's thesis. However, judging by the replies of his readers that were printed in the July 1, 1912 issue of *Hispania*, his call for a stronger union between Latin-American states to prevent European and U.S. aggression did not elicit much support. For example, José C. Borda of Venezuela, wrote, "With or without the Monroe Doctrine, North America will defend us from Europe, as the lion defends the prey which he will devour tomorrow."[37] *The Times* in London was also critical of the plan, arguing that Pérez's "benevolent proposal" overlooked long-standing feuds between the Latin republics and the failure of some states to protect their indigenous population, develop modern health laws, and address other similar matters. The unnamed writer noted that the atrocities promoted by the rubber trade and tolerated by the Peruvian government might legitimately call for outside intervention in order to protect the abused rubber collectors. He concluded: "The fallacy which vitiates Señor Triana's benevolent proposals appears to lie in his assumption of a common and equal measure of civilization and good intentions for all the Latin Republics, an assumption evidently untenable, and which many of those Republics would undoubtedly hasten to repudiate."[38]

Pérez Triana was unmoved by the objections raised by these critics. In an address, "Origins and Significance of the Monroe Doctrine" that he delivered in London on June 19, 1913 and publicized in *Hispania* the following July, he argued that "the acts of violence, usurpation, and spoliation" sometimes ascribed to the Monroe Doctrine, "stand by themselves and do not affect the sanctity of the creed, as the vice of the pontiff does not sully the purity of the doctrine."[39] Underlying the doctrine, he continued, was the "conception that representative government is government of the people, by the people, and for the people." The European powers' current threat to conquer and colonize American territories was likewise a challenge to bring about the end of democratic and representative government. The Monroe Doctrine stood against this intimidation. It was "not the property of the United States, nor the property of America, but of those men who seek liberty, whatever their origin throughout the whole world."[40]

Six months later, Pérez Triana called more explicitly for the Latinization of the Monroe Doctrine in an essay, "The Pan-American Union" published in *Hispania* on February 1, 1914. Here Pérez conceded that although the Monroe Doctrine had protected the hemisphere from European expansion, it had not stopped the United States itself from invading parts of Latin America—actions that had given rise to feelings of distrust that unless dispelled might seriously impair the peace of the continent. It was vital, he continued, to restore cordiality and faith between the United States and the Latin Republics if they were to remain safe from European aggression, and that "all this may be accomplished without difficulty when the United States and other republics of America solemnly declare that conquest is definitively forbidden in the American continent, binding themselves not to practice nor tolerate the conquest of territories in America." The main object of the proposed Pan-American Union was to check the political expansion of Europe and also to end once and forever all future conquest of American territory by American nations. Pérez concluded, "In a few words, it will suffice if the United States and the American republics accept Monroe's declaration carried to its utmost logical development as a fundamental principle of international law for the continent."[41]

In the essays, Pérez made a strong case for the Latinization or Pan-Americanization of the Monroe Doctrine as a way to ensure hemispheric peace in the face of Europe's division into two competing power groups: England, France and Russia versus Germany, Austria and Italy. Events soon bore out his warning of the danger posed by continued militarization in Europe. By the summer of 1914 the continent had become a powder keg that was ignited on June 28, 1914, when heir to the Austro-Hungarian throne, Franz Ferdinand, and his wife, Sophie, were assassinated while visiting Sarajevo, Bosnia—the event that initiated the four-year conflict known as "The Great War."

Colombia, Pérez Triana, and the Great War

On August 7, 1914 three days after Germany invaded Belgium, José Vicente Concha assumed the Colombian presidency. A lawyer, journalist and congressman, Concha was a leading Conservative whose principal concern was to consolidate the hold of his party over the national government. With regard to foreign policy, the pervasive issue he faced even before the outbreak of the Great War was the resolution of Colombia's dispute with the United States over the loss of Panama. After the inauguration of President Woodrow Wilson in 1913 and the completion of the canal the following year, the United States initiated serious negotiations to normalize relations between the two countries. On April 6, 1914, President Wilson signed the Thomson-Urrutia Treaty by which Colombia recognized Panama's independence and the United States expressed "sincere regret" for its actions in 1903, paid Colombia a $25 million indemnity, and granted it special privileges in using the canal. In May, after contentious debate, the Colombian Senate ratified the treaty, confident that whatever its defects, this arrangement would boost public finance, improve the country's financial infrastructure, and make Cartagena and Barranquilla more viable transit ports for inter-ocean trade.[42] Colombians mistakenly believed that this agreement would quickly clear the way for renewed relations with the United States. Unfortunately, the ongoing war in Europe and the resistance of the U.S. Senate to the clause expressing "sincere regret" delayed American ratification until 1921 (and only then with the deletion of the regret clause.)

President Concha's Minister of Foreign Relations, Marco Fidel Suárez, was an experienced diplomat. Suárez had served in the same capacity in previous administrations and was regarded as a distinguished authority on international relations and international law. Following the example of the United States and other Western Hemisphere nations, he proclaimed in August 1914 Colombia's neutrality in the European conflict and imposed a series of resolutions concerning the belligerents that regulated the dispatch of boats, armaments and elements of war, provisioning supplies of food and coal, the permitted length of stay in Colombian waters, and the use of wireless stations.[43] In announcing these policies he was guided by Article V of The Hague Convention, which had been adopted on October 18, 1907, entitled "The Rights and Duties of Neutral Powers and Persons in Case of War on Land." This particular article laid out the ground rules for neutral countries during the Great War.[44]

In addition, Colombia had two other interwoven mechanisms for defending its interests against being drawn into the European war (both strongly supported by Pérez Triana): increasing Pan-American solidarity and transforming the Monroe Doctrine from a U.S. unilateral policy to one embraced by the entire continent. Groundwork for the first option was laid in 1889 when delegates from the Latin American nations and the United States attended the First Pan-American Conference in Washington D.C. Among other actions, they authorized the creation of the Commercial Bureau of the American Republics. At the Second Pan-American Conference, held in Mexico in 1901, the name of the Commercial Bureau was changed to the International Bureau of American Republics, and at the fourth conference, held in Buenos Aires in 1910, the association of nations adopted the name "Union of American Republics," with the Pan American Union (PAU) as its central agency. The fifth Pan-American Conference was scheduled to meet in November 1914 in Santiago, Chile, but that meeting was indefinitely postponed due to the war. As a result, U.S. Treasury Secretary William G. McAdoo's announcement of the Pan-American Financial Conference to meet in Washington, D.C. in May 1915 provided the first opportunity since the onset of the war for Western Hemisphere nations to discuss issues dealing with commerce and public finance.[45]

Concerning the Pan-Americanization of the Monroe Doctrine, reference has already been made to the discussion at the 1907 Hague Convention of the "doctrine" proposed by Luis María Drago which proscribed the right of any country to use military force against another country to collect debts, aimed at de-authorizing the United States and European powers from employing armed intervention to force Latin American countries to pay money owed. Many Latin delegates suggested that this principle was a modification of Monroe's original statement in 1823, but the United States rejected it in favor of adopting the Porter Convention.[46] Nevertheless, it represented an early effort by Latin Americans to transform the idea of the separation of the Western and Eastern Hemispheres embodied in Monroe's proclamation into a multilateral principle rather than one exercised solely by the United States.

This chapter has already outlined the efforts of Pérez Triana in 1912 to support Drago's Doctrine and the Latinization of the Monroe Doctrine. The outbreak of the Great War stirred him to even greater action. In November 1914, he wrote a letter to President Concha. Reprinted in *Hispania*, it was also published in English by the *New York Times* on December 13, 1914, with the headline, "Noted South American Diplomat on Monroe Doctrine of the Future: Santiago Pérez Triana, in a letter to president of Colombia, Declares that Nations of This Continent Must Unite for Resisting Not Only European but Any Other Kind of Aggression."[47]

Pérez began his letter to Concha under the assumption that Colombia would participate in the Fifth Pan-American Congress—unaware that the meeting would be postponed because of the war. "The present European war," he affirmed, "transcends in magnitude and disastrous possibilities all the wars... .It is bringing to the surface traits of barbarism and cruelty which are incredible in this twentieth century of the Christian era." Pérez saw the conflict as the culmination of the balance of power system that European states had adopted, and he warned that no matter which group won, victorious militarism would impose itself for a long time upon the official policies of those nations.

England and France were fighting against German militarism, but they could triumph only with the aid of Russia, and

Russian militarism was no less formidable and odious than that of Germany. The American continents, with the exception of the colonies belonging to the belligerent nations, were outside the political radius of the reign of this barbarism thanks to the Monroe Doctrine. In this connection, Pérez called attention to two points. First, the Monroe Doctrine was not based on altruistic motives but rather solely on the desire of the United States for isolation from the powers of the Eastern Hemisphere and their troubles. Second, although it had prevented the conquest of American territory by European nations, the United States failed to respect the essential equity of the principle, for it had conquered territory by violating the sovereignty of other American nations.

Once Woodrow Wilson became president, Pérez continued, there had been a marked change in White House policy toward Latin America. Wilson had refused to bow to the historical and universal doctrine that it is allowable for a nation to do collectively what for an individual would be criminal, and he had given proof of his sincerity by signing the treaty of April 6, 1914, which made good the injury done to the Republic of Colombia by the Roosevelt administration "in so far as it lay within human power so to do."[48]

With reference to the Monroe Doctrine, in October 1913 President Wilson speaking in Mobile, Alabama declared that the United States would not acquire territory on the American continent by means of war or conquest. The opportunity which now presented itself was to obtain from the United States a solemn ratification of the principle proclaimed at Mobile. If anywhere there was ill feelings toward the United States on account of the past, to allow it to impair judgment would be an unpardonable mistake now that Wilson had erased the past.

Pérez argued that it was extremely important to modify the Monroe Doctrine in order to carry it to its logical development.

That end could be achieved at the Pan-American Congress only if the Latin American nations would affirm that their sovereignty could not be violated by any state in the Western Hemisphere nor by the nations of other continents. Pérez urged President Concha to instruct Colombian delegates attending this congress to raise this idea, thus dignifying the Monroe Doctrine and completing its moral integrity.[49]

Pérez Triana and the First Pan-American Financial Conference, May 24–29, 1915

Concha's reply to Pérez Triana's plea is not recorded. However, with the cancelation of the Pan-American Conference in Santiago, Chile, the forthright positions conveyed by the latter in his letter and in articles published in *Hispania* made him an obvious choice along with Roberto Ancízar to represent Colombia at the first Pan-American Financial Conference announced by U.S. Secretary of the Treasury McAdoo on March 12, 1915.[50] Representatives of 18 Latin American countries and the United States attended the conference which took place in Washington D.C. on May 24–29, 1915.[51] Because Pérez Triana was still suffering the ill effects of his stroke and diabetes, his doctors cautioned him to decline the appointment, warning him that traveling would be "his death sentence."[52] His weak eyesight posed another problem for it had continued to decline, but Cunninghame Graham recalled that Pérez Triana's poor vision did not affect his ability to give an effective oration without referring to notes: "He was endowed with a memory so prodigious that he never revealed the least difficulty in finding the exact word. Still better, the subject and the flow of his speeches were so perfectly clear in his mind that it never appeared that he was speaking something [he had] memorized. All of his sentences seemed spontaneous."[53] In the end,

Gertrude's desire to visit her family in America, and Pérez's eagerness to speak at this meeting despite his health problems determined his decision to accept.[54]

On May 24, 1915 President Wilson opened the conference by welcoming the delegates and expressing "the very high hope, that by this commerce of minds with one another, as well as commerce in goods, we may show the world in part the path to peace."[55] Secretary McAdoo in his following address added his belief that the meeting would enable the Western Hemisphere republics to become a "more homogeneous and powerful moral force for the preservation of peace and the good of humanity."[56] Pérez Triana also made a brief statement which he later titled "The Trusteeship of Liberty." He too emphasized that all the delegates in attendance—representing northern, central and southern republics—were American. Their most important duty, as Europeans turned to slaughter and destruction, was to fortify the inviolability of the continent, "for the pressing hour gives no quarter, and the omission of today may be the irreparable calamity of tomorrow."[57]

For the next four days, the delegates discussed public finance, the monetary situation, the existing banking system, the financing of public improvements and private enterprises, the extension of inter-American markets, the merchant marine, and improving transportation facilities. With regard to emergencies caused by the war, they debated the advantage of creating a permanent hemispheric organization that could deal with such problems as they arose. At length they voted to establish an Inter-American High Commission to which each country would contribute a section of no more than nine persons headed by a cabinet minister in order to carry on the tasks of the international body in all the countries simultaneously. They further resolved that the local members of this commission should be appointed immediately and begin work at once. The organization of this body was a measure of the greatest practical significance since it signaled a movement toward the strengthening of the Pan American Union.[58]

Pérez Triana took a very active role at the conference. He and Ancízar used the meeting as a forum to provide information about Colombia's mines, petroleum, and other natural resources and to emphasize the great opportunities available for capital investment and to urge the settlement of the Panama Treaty issue.[59] Overshadowing these efforts, however, was a speech he presented at the general session on May 25 titled "Inviolability of the Continent."[60]

After being recognized by Secretary McAdoo, Pérez Triana began his talk by observing that his remarks would go beyond the conference's specific purpose of improving financial relations which was one way to achieve the overarching goal of improving the "welfare and the happiness of the peoples of this continent" socially, politically, and internationally. However, since emancipation, he continued, the peoples of this continent had emphasized that they were devoted to democracy and that no outside interference in any form would be tolerated. This position had created a wall-like status which might be defined as "the inviolability of the continent."

Pérez pointed out that during the past twenty-five years, Europe had separated into two rival power groups. While this arrangement had maintained peace, the desire of their rulers to acquire more territory had inevitably turned their attention to the Western Hemisphere which was only protected by a political convention and a pretended inviolability. Pérez Triana warned that since the European powers might look to expansion in America, "We Americans must be prepared to make the inviolability of our continent stronger each day." This statement was met with great applause.

"A house divided against itself soon falls," he continued,

"but ours is not a divided house even though there are small darknesses in corners of the land....Let the nations of the continent, all of them, in a formal and solemn manner, echoing words that have been pronounced in the history of this country by the chief of the executive power of this Nation not long ago, make it manifest...that the borders of the respective nations shall be considered as sacred and never be conquered by force of arms." [Applause]

Addressing the European states, Pérez added that land in the Western Hemisphere was open to people who might come as immigrants but not as conquerors: "All your people may come in their thousands, and in their millions, and we will not only give them a home, but we will crown them with the right of citizenship; but this we tell you, you must come as peaceful multitudes, not as conquering clans. We have no place for your flags."[61]

The "prolonged applause" that followed Pérez Triana's remarks underscored how accurately he was expressing the opinions of the other Latin American delegates. As a result, he earned a second opportunity to address the gathering. At the final banquet, held on the evening of May 29, Secretary McAdoo announced that there would be just two after-dinner addresses—one presented by a representative of the Latin Americans and one by a member of the U.S. delegation. "We [the organizers] finally determined," he explained, "to leave it to our foreign guests to say who should represent them," while he would autocratically appoint a person to speak for the delegates from the United States. "With absolute unanimity," the Latin Americans have chosen "the eloquent gentleman from Colombia who charmed this great conference the other day with an inspired effort." [62]

Pérez Triana began his talk, "On Predatory Imperialism and the Abuse of Sovereignty," by acknowledging the high honor the Latin American delegates had bestowed upon him to speak on their behalf and expressed warmest thanks to the U.S. government for holding the conference and to Secretary McAdoo for the courtesy with which they had been received. He also expressed thanks to the Cabinet and President Wilson, "whom we all consider one of the noblest citizens of mankind [applause and cheers]—a man, a seer, who can see the truth of righteousness and embody them in national policies." [Loud applause]

Before parting," he continued, "we should realize the full significance of our endeavors. Our objective has been that the continents of America should be the home of justice and liberty, and this conference has brought its share to the permanent structure and has paved the way for the future." After reviewing Western Hemisphere history since the United States and the Latin American republics had won their independence, he exhorted Americans of both continents to shoulder their "sacred obligations."

> Although other empires have grown and disappeared, it is our generation's privilege to give a lie to the notions that history repeats itself....Let us achieve prosperity and health, for in material prosperity there is health....In material comfort you will find the development of moral ideals, but of all things let that be the highest aim of our endeavors; let us keep in touch with the treasure of our moral ideals and let us see that those ideas and the ideals which incarnate them become each day more comprehensive and more charitable. [Applause]

Pérez Triana warned that predatory imperialism and the misuse of sovereignty were two dangers that threatened this goal. Predatory imperialism was sporadic and asserted itself where least expected. It looks upon material inferiority as a fault, and it happens frequently that "two men who disagree on everything may come to an easy agreement to seize the property of the third man." The misuse of sovereignty annuls the right of peoples to be governed as they please. In the Western Hemisphere, the sovereignty of each separate section must be sacred, but it should never cloak crime. We can achieve prosperity, he argued, and at the same time maintain intact the treasure of our moral ideals which is the real victory. The American republics must steer a course guided by "these bright stars of hope" and preach this gospel to all nations. "In this respect, at least," he concluded, "I may have managed to interpret the feelings of my fellow delegates"—a statement followed by "great and prolonged applause."[63]

There is no doubt that Pérez Triana had distinguished himself at the Pan-American Financial Conference. As Tad A. Thomson, head of the Legation of the United States in Bogotá, wrote to Minister Suárez on June 1, the appointment of Mr. S. Pérez Triana to represent Colombia "was an extremely happy one....His speeches were listened to with much attention, and they created such a deep impression that it is believed that they will result in the increase of the mutual cordiality and the common welfare of our two Republics."[64]

Pérez Triana continued to serve as a spokesman for the Latin American delegates on a post-conference tour arranged for them by the American government. The tour included visits to Philadelphia, St. Louis, Detroit, and Boston where in each city the group was feted by local dignitaries. At each stop Pérez offered a speech. On June 1 at a banquet hosted by the city of Philadelphia at the Bellevue Stratford Hotel, his topic was "Latin-American Geography—Commerce—Finance." He began by recapitulating the essential geographical conditions of Latin America, and then drew upon the observations gathered on his canoe trip down the Orinoco in 1894 to stress that the natural resources and possibilities of South America might be rivaled but "certainly were not surpassed elsewhere." To develop this potential, he supported three concrete measures that had already been advocated that evening: first, the creation of a bank in the United States that could give financial assistance to industry and commerce in Latin America (and take the place of lost British revenue due to the war); second, the encouragement of private capital to finance agriculture, industry, and the exploitation of forests remembering that each region or nation would have its own peculiar necessities.

Finally, Pérez Triana advocated "broad internationalism." In an oblique reference to the Pan American Union, he suggested that many governments working together for the purposes of humanity under a flag designed as a star of blue upon a field of white could symbolize international cooperation and unity throughout the continent. "Let us hope that, even as 'old Glory' united the sovereign states of this nation in one common effort for democracy, the new flag may unite all the nations of this continent in the same endeavor."[65]

On June 6, Pérez Triana spoke on "The Shadow of the Conquistadores" at a luncheon hosted by the Business Men's League of St. Louis, Missouri. Here he discussed briefly the Spanish and Portuguese conquest of South America and the exploits of Ponce de León and Hernando De Soto in North America. Describing the progress that had occurred in the U.S. plains and forests where "wonderful cities rear their magnificent structures," he observed that it was well to remember the first pioneers who opened the way for luckier generations that have since achieved, "a success which well might be called miraculous." Pérez concluded: "We want our peoples to look to the future as a prodigious canvas, upon which they are to trace, in living deeds of liberty and of justice, their history, which is to be a redemption of mankind."[66]

Chicago was the next stop on the conference delegates' tour. On June 7, Pérez Triana addressed a group of industrialists and manufacturers at the Congress Hotel. His speech for this occasion was titled "On the Memory of Lincoln." He began by saying that as the train carrying the group entered the state of Illinois, there arose in his mind "majestic and prophetic, the figure of the martyred president, then whom no nobler and no greater man was ever born on this Western Continent, that we call America." He urged his audience to see how they could strengthen and fortify this home of liberty—a goal that might be best attained by the cooperation of commerce and industry. Noting that the war had disrupted the economies of South America, Pérez suggested that Chicago bankers could help them to recover by extending money and credit to merchants and industrialists. In return, they would find a "very vast field for the consumption of their manufactured products." To achieve success North Americans should imitate Europeans and sell what Latin Americans wanted to buy rather than continue their traditional strategy of offering products that they thought their customers ought to buy. Pérez closed his talk by inviting the financiers and industrialists to visit South America so that the co-operation that he was advocating might become each day a greater reality.[67]

On June 9, Pérez Triana delivered his fourth talk in Detroit at a banquet sponsored by that city's Board of Commerce. Aptly calling it "On Speech Inflicting and Speech Enduring," he asked permission to wander from Pan-Americanism, financial and otherwise, to discuss other fields of human endeavors on the grounds that his colleagues had heard his ideas many times and that "there would be grave peril in the tenth re-infliction." Despite this disclaimer, he again focused on the importance of Pan-Americanism and its supreme aim: the joint effort between north and south to seek liberty and justice through democracy.[68]

On June 12 Pérez Triana presented perhaps his most important speech, "On the Monroe Doctrine," in Boston, the final stop of the tour.[69] At a banquet in the Algonquin Club sponsored by the Boston Chamber of Commerce, he began by observing that because of the upsets to long-established harmonies of economic intercourse caused by the European War, the Pan-American Financial Conference had a attained a transcendent and historic character in the search for global readjustments and new forms of trade. Since the United States had a surplus of capital and "the Latin sections of the Continent possess incalculable sources of natural wealth as yet untouched," the conference had raised the possibility of forging a link between the two regions, essentially creating an economic partnership with the United States to replace that which the Latin American countries had formerly held with Europe and especially with England.

Pérez once again stated his conviction that the Monroe Doctrine had saved the Western Hemisphere from European conquest and must now be strengthened and rendered unassailable by the joint efforts of all American nations. To secure wholehearted support for the Monroe Doctrine throughout the hemisphere, "it should be enacted and covenanted among all the nations of the continent that the territory of the American nations is no longer a subject for conquest *either from within* [emphasis mine] or from without the continent."

To soften this obvious condemnation of aggressive U.S. action in the Caribbean, Pérez Triana noted that President Wilson had already proclaimed "internal inviolability to be the essential foundation of inviolability from the outside." With stirring words, Pérez extolled the need for mutual cooperation: "Look-

ing backward to the history of this land and to the written pre-
cepts of its collective efforts, and to the achievements realized,
we of the southern half, believe in our hearts that such are your
guiding principles. We do not call you perfect, for no man and
no nation has ever been perfect. But we believe in your sincerity of purpose as you must believe in ours; and so we may
go hand in hand toward the rising sun."[70]

Pérez's speech amounted to a proposal that the Monroe
Doctrine should be transformed into a hemispheric union that
would eventually become the Organization of American States.
Arnold Peters, U.S. Assistant Secretary of the Treasury, responded to this suggestion by assuring the assembly that President Wilson was giving the international situation the most
careful deliberation. He added, "It is a singular privilege, there-
fore, to express confidence, as I see you gentlemen here
tonight, that the president may count on the unbounded loyalty
of those who never fail at such a time as this, the patriotic citizens of Boston."[71]

Following Pérez Triana's return to London, the editors of
Hispania published in the July 1, 1915 issue a report on the
activities of the financial conference. Summarizing the nature
of the meeting and the countries that were represented in
Washington D.C., they went on to lament that the European
press had not paid sufficient attention to the work that had been
achieved, especially since the efforts of the delegates had been
to mitigate the ongoing war's impact on American commerce.
The conference had lasted only a few days, but much had been
accomplished with regard to improving maritime communication between the members of the Pan American Union. In
addition, Paul M. Warburg, a member of the U.S. Federal Re-
serve Board, had affirmed that his country had $1,890,000,000
available at hand as credit that could be extended to the southern republics to ameliorate the loss of European trade.

The principal merit of the conference, however, lay in its moral implications. As President Wilson had stated in his inaugural address, the countries of the Western Hemisphere were cementing a policy of permanent peace, while the richest and most powerful countries in Europe were engaged in a destructive war. *Hispania's* editorial emphasized Pérez Triana's important role in expressing the aspirations of Latin American peoples and how his speeches had been praised in the U.S. press. This success had been achieved due to his many hours of meditation and study over the last years. "Those of us who have worked with him take pride in the rightful place he has assumed while other more exalted individuals who have wanted to hurt him had fallen into legitimate obscurity that covers their pettiness and incurable blindness."[72] In the August 1 issue of *Hispania*, Pérez Triana reprinted his speech on the Monroe Doctrine which he had presented to the Boston Chamber of Commerce.[73]

In his essay "Pan-American Financial Conference" which was included in *The Pan-American Financial Conference of 1915,* Pérez Triana provided a more complete summary of developments in Washington. He returned to the idea that the Western Hemisphere's status of being off-limits to European powers had been "one of the determining causes of the present war." While England and France were acquiring colonies in Africa and Asia during the nineteenth century, Germany had been concentrating on unifying its state in Europe. Once this goal had been achieved, from 1870 onward the Kaiser had focused his ambitions on catching up with England and France by seizing overseas possessions. Given his mindset the Western Hemisphere and especially southern Brazil would have been an appealing target. Because of the Monroe Doctrine, however, "political expansion in America was out of the question."

In his address to Pan-American Financial Conference delegates, President Wilson had asserted that the United States was
prepared to assist Latin American countries whose trade had
been disrupted by the outbreak of the war. By 1915 European
supplies to Latin America, financially speaking, had practically
come to a standstill, and under those circumstances, Pérez concluded, it was only natural that the United States and the other
nations of the Americas should meet in council to seek what
measures should be adopted to deal with the situation.[74] Speaking at the opening of the session, Mr. Frank A. Vanderlip, President of the National City Bank of New York, had affirmed
that the U.S. national banks had "perfectly enormous capital
for the expansion of loans, probably enough to provide loans
of two or three billion dollars." Whether U.S. manufacturing
possibilities were of equal proportions was less assured, but
Pérez Triana asserted that "there would seem to be no doubt
as to the marvelous elasticity of American industrial resources."[75]

Thus, the conference had come at a most important time,
and while it was not infrequent to hear Europeans complaining
that the United States was selfishly taking advantage of the
Old World conflict by seizing markets long held by England
and France, in fact, as Pérez pointed out, the United States was
really helping to save European interest in Latin America by
preventing the countries from going bankrupt. With regard to
manufactured goods, if the European manufacturer was unable
to supply his customers, the latter could hardly be blamed for
seeking necessary goods elsewhere. Pérez Triana concluded:
"Pan-Americanism has come to signify something beyond financial relations....It has come to stand for freedom through
democracy....The struggle in Europe is fundamentally between democracy and absolutism, and the sympathies of the
peoples of America are with Britain and her allies."[76]

In a second essay, "Pan-Americanism," also included in *The Pan-American Financial Conference of 1915*, Pérez Triana sought both to further define the term and to show its relationship with the Monroe Doctrine. He began by conceding that no precise conception of what Pan-Americanism was had received widespread acceptance. On the most basic level it was held to mean "America for Americans." But how did one determine who was "American?" It could not be narrowed by ethnicity (there were Americans of all races), by birth (millions of Americans were born outside of America), by religion (there were Americans professing every variety of religion), or by language (in addition to English, Spanish and Portuguese there were innumerable forms of speech in the New World). Pan-Americanism was different from Pan-Germanism, Pan-Slavism, and Pan-Islam—the first two of which were grounded essentially on race, language and tradition, while Pan-Islam had a religious connotation.[77]

Pérez asserted that the present Pan-American movement was not based fundamentally on geography but on the political independence of the American continent. It did not involve economic independence because commerce and finance were international and because both European and American countries benefitted equally from trans-Atlantic trade. "A Pan-Americanism that assumed for the two American continents a divergence of interests with Europe was not the one incarnate in the present movement."[78] The fundamental difference between America and Europe was that the path of liberty and justice was not beset in the former with the pitfalls of tradition that existed in the latter. "Each American nation wants to lead its own life independently, free from European or inter-American aggressions."[79]

Pérez argued that Pan-Americanism as a diplomatic alliance of all the American nations had never been a matter for serious

discussion, and that before the present conflict, the United
States had been just as economically dependent on European
financing as its Latin neighbors. At the present time, however,
thanks to the war, U.S. national banks now held an enormous
surplus of funds. The true bond of union lay not in political alliances or international confederations, but in "the firm resolve
and indomitable purpose of the peoples of America, to maintain the Continent inviolate for the practice of Democracy, as
the only road to Liberty."[80]

It had been suggested that the United States would not obtain cooperation from the Latin nations, but the facts developing each day spoke otherwise. It had also been said that the
Monroe Doctrine had been a gigantic "bluff," that Europe
would no longer tolerate it, and that the United States sooner
or later would abandoned this traditional policy. To the contrary, as Pérez pointed out, the Monroe Doctrine had saved the
continent up to the present and was not likely to be discarded
in the future. To support his position, he cited "The True Monroe Doctrine," a speech delivered by ex-Secretary of State and
then-President of the American Society of International Law,
Elihu Root, at the society's eighth annual meeting in Washington in April 1914. After reviewing the role of the Doctrine in
nineteenth-century diplomacy— when Spain, France, England,
and Germany on different occasions conceded that they had
no intention of acquiring territory in the Western Hemisphere—Root observed that in ratifying The Hague Arbitration
Conventions of 1907, the U.S. Senate had stated that nothing
in its ratification could be construed as the United States re-
linquishing its traditional attitude towards purely American
questions.[81] Pérez concluded that the lesson of American history is eloquent and clear: the Monroe Doctrine would remain,
and Pan-Americanism would grow and flourish for the good
of humanity.[82]

In summary, between 1909 and 1915, Santiago Pérez Triana, through his editorship of *Hispania*, his many essays, and his multiple activities at the First Pan-American Financial Conference, emerged as one of the most eloquent and respected supporters of Pan-American cooperation and the Latinization of the Monroe Doctrine. Drawing on his European experiences and his remarkable oratorical gifts, he had become a spokesperson for the nations in Latin America in their bid to be recognized as significant players on the international scene. These efforts were not without great personal cost. As we shall see, his health steadily declined after his return to England.

— CHAPTER —

6

Support for the Allied Cause in the Great War, 1914–1916

*"Hatred is an incapacity in peoples to be great and
a lack of merit in men in order to be free."*
SANTIAGO PÉREZ TRIANA

érez's support for the Allies in the Great War began before his participation in the Pan-American Financial
Conference and continued until his death in May 1916.
He had lived many years in Germany and had learned to love
it, but the Germany he had experienced was composed of beer
drinking, students, music, thinkers, legends, romantic ballades,
clubs, simplicity, generosity and dreams. The Reich's declaration of war and its early conduct in the fighting presented a
picture in stark contrast to these memories. When confronted
with the German onslaught on Belgium, the horror of unnec-
essary massacres, the blasphemous invocation of the name of
God, and the seeding of terror and pain, Pérez willingly spoke
out as a prophet—not against the German people who were
the first victims of Germany militarism but against their irre-
sponsible leaders.[1]

In a letter to the editor of the *Times* that was published on
September 17, 1914 under the headline "The War and the Law

of Nations," Pérez Triana wrote that with their invasion of Belgium, Germany and Austria-Hungary had blatantly defied Article 44 of Convention IV of the Second Hague Peace Conference agreement which proscribed "belligerents to force the population of an occupied territory to give information about the other belligerent army or about its means of defense." Since "forcing" might include anything from terrorizing and torturing to killing, their actions had stirred "the conscience of mankind throughout the world into feelings of awe-stricken indignation." Already Pérez believed that the Allies would eventually emerge victorious. He urged Britain to notify the enemy that special courts would try the officers who permitted the alleged outrages against the elementary laws of humanity. Further, he believed that the neutral nations should demand the application of this principle to all the belligerents, and that the Allies should bind themselves to mete out the same treatment to any transgressors of their own, should any arise in the course of the war. "This war, sir," he concluded, "recognizes no neutral in its consequences, and the fate of all nationalities the world over is being determined on the battlefields of Central Europe."[2]

In the ensuing months, Pérez made clear his support for the Allies in three other ways. First, in November 1914, after Germany had declared war, he attempted to supply horses to the British army by purchasing animals in Argentina and Uruguay. Second, he published his influential book, *Some Aspects of the War* in July 1915. Third, on returning to London after attending the Pan-American Financial Conference, he wrote pro-Allies editorials for *Hispania* and gave speeches to various groups in England about the importance of Latin America in what had become a global crisis. This chapter will discuss these activities after a brief review of the official reaction in Colombia on receipt of news of the conflict's outbreak in August 1914.

Once Germany had declared war, Colombia's foreign minister, Marco Fidel Suárez, following the example of other Western Hemisphere countries, announced a policy of scrupulous neutrality. Given that Colombian legislation protecting the freedom of the press was quite liberal, some periodicals launched violent attacks against the belligerents in spite of Suárez's circular to the editors on November 17, 1914 reminding them that "absolute freedom of the press does not mean the absence of duties or responsibilities....A state of absolute indifference is impossible, but sympathies and antipathies may express themselves in the rational form of truth in the respectful form of courtesy and in the Christian form of benevolence."[3]

The need for his admonition was clear, for at the opening of the war, Colombian public opinion was sharply divided concerning the motives and prospects of the belligerent sides. Due to its support of Panamanian independence, its military invasions of the Dominican Republic, Haiti, and Nicaragua, and the failure of the Senate to ratify the Thomson-Urrutia Treaty, the United States had not won for itself many friends. At the same time German propaganda and economic penetration had made considerable inroads in Colombia during the years immediately preceding the war. German capital was heavily invested in mining and agriculture. A German company, *Compañía Hanseática del Río León* was raising bananas on the Gulf of Darien, a location of immense strategic importance owing to its proximity to the Caribbean entrance to the newly completed Panama Canal. The German ambassador to Colombia, Herr Kracker von Schwartzenfeldt was an able promoter of his country's objectives, and the Germans also had a champion in the fiery Conservative, Laureano Gómez, who consistently supported their cause in his pro-clerical newspaper, *La Unidad.*[4] For example, in an editorial titled "The Convenience

of a German Victory" he wrote: "Several times we've argued
in this newspaper that Latin American nations should lean toward Germany in the present conflict because the victory of
that nation would favor the autonomy and development of
South American nations presently menaced by Yankee imperialism," and he added that the principal nations allied against
Germany—England and France—had in recent years abused
Colombia and her sister republics.[5]

Despite these factors, many Colombians were aware of the
ominous portent posed by war between the great European
powers and favored the Allies. Illustrative of their concern was
an article titled "La conflagración Europea" (The European
War), written by "Calibán" and published in *La Linterna*, the
most prominent Liberal newspaper of Tunja, on August 7,
1914.[6] Calibán described the conflict that had just broken out
as a "horrendous catastrophe the scope of which had not occurred in recent centuries....Twenty million men attacking one
another with uncontainable fury, driven by secular and racial
hatreds that can only end with the definitive destruction of Europe, or perhaps the total ruin of the old Western Civilization."
Although he predicted the eventual victory of the Triple En-
tente (France, Russia, England) over the Triple Alliance (Germany, Austria, Italy), he feared that the aftermath of the war
would expose Europe to forces of unbridled anarchy and socialism.[7]

Living in London, Pérez Triana could openly express support for the Allies without violating his country's neutrality. In
November 1914, at about the same time that he wrote his letter
to President Concha, he may have embarked on a more concrete scheme to help the Allies, but there are two conflicting
versions of this effort. According to Sanín Cano, in the early
months of the war, Pérez Triana, with his gift for influencing
people and his cordial relations with journalists and politicians,

succeeded in getting a concession to supply horses from South America to the British army. Since he had no expertise in judging horses and could not possibly travel to Argentina, he asked his friend Cunninghame Graham, whose horsemanship was well known and whom Santiago saw riding every morning in Hyde Park, to take charge of this aspect of the endeavor. Don Roberto accepted the charge and undertook a voyage in early 1915 to Argentina and Uruguay to locate the animals.

While at sea, Graham met a Spaniard who owned stores and commission houses in both Hamburg and Montevideo. Don Roberto, happy to find a passenger with whom he could speak Spanish and unaware that the Spaniard was sympathetic to the German cause, spoke freely about his mission. Unbeknownst to him, the Spaniard did not delay many hours in advising his agents to buy as many horses as they could knowing that they would be doing a great service for Germany. As a result, when Don Roberto arrived in Uruguay, he learned that all the available horses had already been purchased by the Spaniard. Advised of this development, Graham did not even visit Buenos Aires but returned to London as soon as possible. Sanín Cano notes that Pérez Triana had enlisted several friends in his scheme, and on learning of Don Roberto's failure, he was furious at the man's imprudence and naivety. For nearly a year, he and Don Roberto were no longer on speaking terms, and the impasse was not resolved until Pérez Triana was on his deathbed.[8]

The difficulty with accepting this account of a break in the friendship between Pérez and Graham is that the latter's biographers, Watts and Davies, offer a completely different description of the effort to purchase South American horses for the European war. According to Watts and Davies, Don Roberto tried to volunteer for the British army but was told that at age 62 he was too old for active service. Instead the War Office appointed him president of a commission that was to travel to South America to purchase as many suitable animals as possible. Towards the end of November 1914, Graham sailed to Uruguay and Argentina accompanied by a number of army officers. On arriving in Montevideo, he went on to Buenos Aires. In both countries the horses had to be rounded up, ridden, inspected, sorted, and branded. Once their manes were shorn off, they were driven to pasture to await shipment. Graham's job was to select and buy more than 2,000 of the animals.[9] As A. F. Tschiffely observes, "He [Graham] was on a mission he detested, for the very idea of taking horses out of their peaceful grazing grounds in order to send them to be slaughtered on the battlefields in France sickened his heart. Still he felt that he was doing his duty."[10]

Graham returned to England with the horses at the end of May 1915. On the way there his ship was torpedoed by a German submarine in the English Channel. Fortunately, with great presence of mind, the ship's captain managed to run the vessel onto a sandy beach, safely landing all the passengers and horses. Having completed his mission, Graham used his influence to obtain a commission in the army for Joseph Conrad's son, Borys, and then turned to writing a series of sketches and essays for the *English Review* and the *Nation*.[11]

It is virtually impossible to reconcile the differences in these two accounts. The fact that Graham did acquire the horses is well documented, while Sanín Cano's version appears to rely on what Pérez had told him. Perhaps Graham refused in some way to supply Pérez and his associates some of the promised horses, but for whatever reason a rift between the two friends did occur, and only Sanín Cano seems to have recorded this explanation.[12]

On May 7, 1915, just before delegates to the Pan-American Financial Conference were to assemble in Washington D.C., a

German submarine sank the British liner *Lusitania* off the coast of southern Ireland causing the deaths of 1,959 people on board including 128 U.S. civilians. The unrelenting German strategy of U-boat attacks on merchant and passenger ships had brought the United States to the brink of declaring war several times and underscored the country's diplomatic efforts to win solidarity with other hemispheric countries. Pérez Triana, drawing on the experience of his years as a student in Germany, again proved to be a solid supporter of the Allied cause. In July 1915 he published a collection of 13 essays in English (originally written in Spanish) in a book, *Some Aspects of the War*, that was unswervingly critical of the German war effort.[13] In one chapter titled, "Why a Spanish-American should not be Pro-German," he wrote:

> The tragedy of Belgium, attacked with cold deliberation and torn from limb to limb by the troops of his Majesty the Kaiser, has staggered humanity; it stands out against the horizon like a hellish vision of agony and of shame for the whole human race. With what right would a Spanish-American, identified through his support with Prussia's unspeakable acts in Belgium...demand a better fate for his own country...when, if Prussia is victorious in her fatal and inexorable evolution, the surging wave of German voracity reaches his own native land?

Pérez added that by continuing to study in Germany, the "young South American" was implicitly endorsing German policy, and he ended by stating that there could be no neutrality in this matter. "We must all sink or swim together. The tempest rages furiously beneath a sky vivid with the lightning flash in this hour of destiny."[14]

In another chapter, "The Name of God and the War," Pérez denounced the Kaiser's habit of "ordering God Almighty to form in the ranks with his other servants" to fight for the Junkers and their privileges as "the most audacious and glaring form of blasphemy."[15] In a third chapter, "The Settlement of Peace," he warned of the dangers of Prussian admirers among the Allies. "There are Prussians in Britain and France who never spoke a word of German," he wrote, "and if the dictation of peace terms is left to such men, no matter which way the victory goes, the desolating competition in armaments, which is used to tame the masses down to a life limited by taxation, will be extended to the rest of the world."[16]

In the U.S. press, Pérez Triana's book and his sentiments received high praise. On August 29, 1915, a reviewer for the *New York Times* wrote that his attitude was especially significant because "he is a Colombian and to a certain extent speaks for Latin America." Moreover, it continued, he was a man who had attended a German university in his youth and thus had experienced firsthand "the privileged ruffianism of Prussian soldiers in the streets of Berlin which disgusted him."[17] The critic for the *Saturday Review* observed that there were many parts of the book worth reading, especially since "Señor Triana is one of the most deeply informed men on some subjects and a personality whose force and charm has been felt and recognized by all his friends."[18]

In the months following his return from the United States, Pérez Triana's health declined precipitously as his doctors had predicted. He was already nearly blind, and in addition to his worsening heart condition, an open foot wound complicated by diabetes failed to heal. As Louis Bonafoux would later report in the Madrid *Heraldo*, he was dying slowing "bit by bit (*"moría a pedazos"*)."[19] Undeterred, he kept busy until his death by editing *Hispania* and writing articles to support the Allies, condemn the Germans, and promote a Pan-Americanized Monroe Doctrine.[20]

After the August 1 issue of *Hispania,* the journal did not publish in September and October due to a "reorganization," but the November issue included Pérez Triana's article on Pan-Americanism and contributions by other writers organized under the categories of "Arts and Letters," "General Articles," "The International Situation," and "News of the War." In December the *revista* featured two editorials by Pérez and articles by Sanín Cano, William Archer, and Manuel Kant. Monthly issues of *Hispania* published between January and June of 1916 continued this general format.

On April 8, 1916 Pérez Triana wrote a letter that was published in the Bogotá periodical, *Gil Blas,* in which he predicted that an ominous future lay ahead for Latin America beyond the end of the Great War. Once peace was declared, he explained, the European powers would seek to replenish resources lost during the fighting, and they would again look to Latin America. Colombia and other South American countries had cattle, minerals including iron, coal, and especially petroleum. "Can we believe," he warned, "that the world will respect our territorial rights?" His implication was that Latin American governments must be prepared to resist future exploitation of its natural resources from these outside powers.[21]

Pérez Triana delivered his last public address, "The Neutrality of Latin America" on February 10, 1916, at the 93rd dinner of the Political and Economic Circle of the National Liberal Club in London. Cunninghame Graham, as president of the club, introduced Pérez as a man "well known to many of us here and very well known to the London public in general."

> A Latin-American himself, he is married to an English-American, and he has chosen to make his home

amongst us in this country. Speaking, as he does,
both languages with equal fluency and perfection,
he is able to deal with such a question more effi-
ciently—which is, I think, the slang word of the
day—than perhaps any public man in the two hemispheres; and he has a subject that not only such a
speaker as himself, but almost anyone, could make
an interesting address about.[22]

Pérez Triana began his talk by describing Latin America as
19 nations "only born yesterday" that came of age in 1907
when they were invited to the Second Hague Convention to
"sit in council, on equal terms, with the great Powers of the
world." At The Hague the Latinos played their part worthily,
casting their votes for "justice, for humanity, for equality of
opportunity for all nations, great and small, for the sanctity of
treaties, for the protection of non-combatants in time of war,
for the reduction of the unavoidable horrors of war....and for
the submission to arbitration of all differences and disputes"—
all principles that Britain and her allies were upholding. He
continued, "Whether those of us born outside the fighting nations recognize it or not, the fact remains, that we are all belligerents for in this sense, there are no neutrals, as there can
be no options when the floodtide invades the premises; we
must all sink or swim."[23]

Recounting Spanish America's fight for independence from
Spain in the early nineteenth century, Pérez emphasized that
the nations today continue "to live their own life in sympathy
with the Mother Country." He went on to note that Britain's
contribution to their survival in terms of diplomacy and loans
had developed over the nineteenth century into an active participation in the industrial and commercial development of
Latin America. Other European rivals in commerce, industry,

and finance had come at a later day. Eagerness to invest often led to bargains with ruthless official iniquity, which, in turn, signified blood-stained oppression at home and punctually paid maturities in Europe.

The independent nations of America today enjoyed neutrality, he continued, but neutrality was no protection from loss or disaster; it was only a shield against intentional violence and actual warfare: "Our governments may tell us 'we are neutral,' but our consciences are free. In some wars such as the so-called religious and dynastic wars that have devastated Europe over the centuries, an outsider might well remain impartial, but when principles and not plunder constitute the main issue, impartiality becomes impossible. As far as opinion is concerned, Latin America today cannot be an outsider despite official political neutrality, for the issues are vital to all mankind."[24]

Pérez urged his English audience to remember that good opinion from even the smallest country is valuable and that it was important to insure that public opinion in Latin America be pro-British and not pro-German. Latin Americans knew that a victorious Germany would bring a conquering Germany to their lands. They too had Prussians born and bred in their midst who needed watching. German propaganda was widespread in Latin America as in all neutral lands; "She subsidizes newspapers, floods the country with books, pamphlets, leaflets, postcards and uses songs and motion pictures to her advantage...relying on the gullibility of the multitudes and on the efficacy of persistent reiteration."[25]

Pérez concluded that truth must "resound like a clarion blast, in neutral countries, each day, at dawn and at sunset. It must stir the consciences of men and sweep away the mists of German lies." German activities must be counteracted. Britain preaches and practices liberty and champions the small nations. She did not start this war, and there must and shall be victory—"for the liberty of the World and the dignity of Man."[26]

A question and answer period followed these remarks with each speaker limited to five minutes. Mr. John Hatfield pointed out that there were possibly thousands of Irish living and making their homes throughout Spanish America and suggested that they would be able to counteract on their own the poisonous influence of Germany. Geographer Reginald Enock followed. Drawing on his considerable experience working in Ecuador, he pointed out that a small group of cultivated members of the upper class in Latin America, forming less than perhaps ten percent of the population, ruled over millions of illiterate and poverty-stricken Indians. Enock suggested that these upper classes should be improving the lives of the enormous bulk of ordinary people far more quickly than they were doing. Nevertheless, he was glad to hear that Latin America's elite supported the British, and he suggested that Anglo-Saxons should cultivate the Latin American countries far more than previously, "both for their own benefit and our own, as I am sure we have something to learn from each other." This statement was followed by applause.[27]

Enock's very positive comments were followed by more skeptical ones. A Mr. Richards pointed out that there were "standing complaints in the newspapers and elsewhere that the case of Great Britain is not sufficiently advertised in the various neutral countries." He noted that North Americans had rejected a renewed British propaganda campaign on the grounds that they "would rather form their own judgment" than receive English impressions. He agreed with Mr. Enock that South American republican opinion was confined to the comparatively few who belonged to the upper and commercial classes, and he suggested that Pérez had failed to suggest a way for improving propaganda methods: "I am asking for information when I say:

Has Señor Triana any suggestion to make as to any methods he would use for getting at those classes in South American republics which may be useful, in the way of increasing their zeal in behalf of the allies? If he has any method let us have it and adopt it. If he has not, then I am afraid we are no better off."[28]

Pérez Triana conceded that the upper or cultured class in Latin America might not be very numerous "but then the rudder of the ship is not very large, and it guides the ship. Mr. Richards' question, 'Have I any method better than those employed so far?' is far more important." Pérez answered this query by citing an experience during his recent trip to the United States. While attending a banquet in Pittsburgh, he had sat next to Mr. Samuel H. Church, a man well known in England who had written a crushing reply to certain German professors. After the meal the diners had begun singing a variety of songs which included, to Pérez's surprise, the nationalistic German song "Wacht Am Rhein." When he asked Mr. Church why such a song would be sung, Church replied, "My dear fellow, it startles me as much as it does you; but remember that there are from 300,000 to 400,000 Germans in these parts." Pérez observed:

> In America, people have other preoccupations besides the war. The propaganda I suggest is to call their attention to the vital importance of the issues and to destroy the German lies. One hears abroad that the English are committing cruelties against the Germans. What I suggest with regard to propaganda is not that a man should go out in the street, take off his coat, and shout "Rule Britannia;" that is emotion, not argument. I want that man to sit down, take up his pen, and write about "The freedom of the sea" and everything that is not clear in men's minds,

and show them that England is right, not because it
is England, but because it is right. Do not defend
the cause by shouting, but by argument....I say that
the opinion of the smallest group, even in South
America, where we are told that so few thousands
constitute the leading classes—even that opinion is
worth having, and it should not become pro-German. If there is someone here who wants to study
the question of propaganda in Latin America, I am
his man, because I know the country, and I pay
cash—that is to say, can suggest practical action.
[Loud laughter and applause][29]

Graham underscored Pérez's comments by adding that
when he was in Argentina, he used to go out riding with the
gauchos (or *ponchos* as he called them), and that most of them
watched German-made films shown in small towns. These
films always depicted the British and French as running away
from the battlefield, defeated. "When I said to my ponchos,
'That, of course, is a lie,' they always said to me, 'It is in the
cinema,' in precisely the same way as people here say 'It is in
the *Daily Mail*,' and they believed it." Graham concluded, "We
have got to do something practical to counteract the lies of
Germany and to rope in—you will excuse a professional
metaphor—to corral those sympathies and to dispel those false
views which Germany is putting forward."[30]

Mr. Fisher Unwin, a publisher, followed stating that he had
first met Señor Triana at The Hague Peace Conference in
1899.[31] He had high praise for Cunninghame Graham for he
was one of the few Englishmen who know both Spanish and
Spanish America. "I wish there were hundreds more of such;
it would help to bring Spanish America more into line with
Britain and her allies; and then we should be in a better posi-

tion than we are in today. We must look upon South America and the Southern American Republics as our friends and allies for many years to come."[32] He then proposed a toast to Cunninghame Graham who afterwards requested that Pérez Triana say a few words to the group in Spanish. Pérez agreed, stating: "I have already spoken perhaps too much but....I hope the few words I have said tonight may add something to your information, and perhaps I may not be too daring in hoping that it may make a lasting impression for good. Viva Inglaterra."[33]

This account of Pérez Triana's address to the National Liberal Club is informative for it accurately reveals not only his efforts to explain South America's situation during the Great War, but also British attitudes about South America in early 1916. Moreover, it was to be his last public appearance.

Pérez continued to correspond with friends and colleagues in both Europe and Colombia. In 1914, when he learned that José María Quijano Wallis was planning to write his memoire, he wrote to him from Paris offering to contribute a prologue for the proposed book. Born in 1847 Quijano Wallis was a lawyer, diplomat, politician, historian and member of the Radical Liberal faction. Between 1878 and 1881 he served as Colombia's chargé d'affaires and consul general in the Kingdom of Italy, and in 1913 he was elected president of the Colombian Academy of Jurisprudence. Quijano accepted Pérez' offer, but the latter was unable to complete the task. When Quijano published his *Memorias: autobiográficas, histórico-políticos y de character social* in 1915, he included Pérez's original letter as a supplement to a prologue written by Nicolás Esguerra. Addressing Quijano as "My dear Doctor and friend," Pérez wrote that he considered Quijano an integral part of his father's Liberal generation even though he was somewhat younger in years, and that he had left a "brilliant, sympathetic, honorable and fertile mark in his collaboration with the work of the Republic." He praised Quijano as a "fighter for liberal principals…and for the great Liberal Party which incarnated the hope of progress and true liberty for the Republic, purified by defeat and by maturity" and he expressed confidence that political parties that had been wrongly suppressed in Colombia would "surge again glorious and powerful for the good of the Republic."[34]

In March 1916 Pérez Triana moved his family to his country house in Riverdale Cowley, Middlesex—a home that was as luxurious as his elegant residence in Regent's Park. Now completely blind and suffering from heart problems and diabetes, he went to Riverdale Cowley to die. According to Sanín Cano, with his end in sight, Pérez urged Gertrude to contact Cunninghame Graham since he did not wish to die without reconciling with his English friend. Graham did come to see him, and while no one witnessed their encounter, after he had departed there was no doubt that all animosity that had arisen between them had been resolved. A few days later Pérez died on May 23, 1915 at the age of 58—his father's birthday. He was buried in St. Mary's Roman Catholic Cemetery in Kensal Green, London.

After Pérez Triana's burial, his widow, having settled his affairs in England, returned to the United States on January 17, 1917 traveling with her son Sonny and her maid on the steamship "Finland." Gertrude O'Day established her residence at No. 65 Central Park West in New York City. On May 17, 1919 she married Julian F. Meredith, a previously twice-married artist, who resided in Greenwich, Connecticut.[35]

On September 12, 1918 Sonny, now 20 years old, registered with the Selective Service Board, listing his occupation as "student." He was not drafted into the U.S. Army, since the Great War was nearing its conclusion, but unfortunately he appears to have been a victim of the war's accompanying influenza pandemic. On November 21, 1919, having been ill for only 24 hours, Sonny died suddenly due to a hemorrhage brought on by a severe cold.[36]

7

Assessing the Life and Career of Santiago Pérez Triana

"Each age has its way of using life. One must discover this and employed it as fully and nobly as possible."

SANTIAGO PÉREZ TRIANA

The purpose of this book has been to restore Santiago Pérez Triana's place in Colombian history by presenting an extensive examination of his life, his career, and especially his impact on inter-American relations based on archival sources and his own numerous publications. As we have seen, he was well known in his lifetime, and the news of his death prompted a deep sense of loss in Colombia, the United States, and Europe. Nevertheless, as years went by, the memory of his significance faded to the extent that the 100th anniversary of his death on May 23, 2016 passed unnoticed in Colombia and elsewhere. The goals of this chapter are to assess Pérez Triana's historical importance in the first two decades of the twentieth century as a Colombian man of letters and South American diplomat and to offer an explanation as to why he is virtually unknown in Colombia today.

Given his celebrity in 1916, it is not surprising that the news of Pérez Triana's death prompted lavish obituaries published in Colombia's national newspapers; *El Tiempo, Diario Nacional,* and *Gaceta Republicana* reported the sad event on May 25, 1916 with *El Gráfico* doing the same on June 3. *El Tiempo*'s notice reflected the assertion expressed in the other periodicals when it stated that Pérez's passing "has deprived our homeland of one of its most important intellectual figures and cut short in an unexpected manner the victorious career of that worthy man who by force of talent and art made his name famous in Europe and America and covered all of Colombia with glorious splendor."[1]

G. J. Rodríguez began his tribute in *El Gráfico* by pointing out the difficulty of condensing the essence of so vast a personality into a single place. He predicted that in the future, others would write more about his literary production and his work as a pacifist. Rodriguez observed that Pérez Triana "had been a constant preoccupation" of his contemporaries, some of whom found fault with him while others admired his enormous talent, his books, his speeches, his words, and his manner of gracefully emerging from troublesome situations. Despite his alleged defects, Rodriguez continued, Pérez Triana was a true nationalist, for in his later years he focused his writings on Colombia: "His distant vision helped him to distinguish it, to know it better. He remained very much informed of its situation, needs, and problems and suggested ways to overcome them."[2]

With the headline, "Santiago P. Triana Dead: He Advocated that Western Hemisphere be Retained by Americans," the *New York Times* published its obituary on May 26, 1916. This brief piece noted that Pérez Triana was a native Colombian and the son of a former president of that country. He had served as Colombian minister to England among other diplomatic capacities, and at the time of his death, he was one of the world's best-known South Americans. The obituary cited his partici-

Santiago Pérez Triana in 1916

pation in the Pan-American Financial Conference and remarked that his address to that assembly had emphasized the
importance for all Americans from both the North and the
South to join together to stress "that the rest of the world
[must] come to understand that the Western Hemisphere is to
be retained by Americans and will not be permitted to be made
the victim of territorial acquisitions by European Powers."[3]

Europeans also observed Pérez Triana's passing. The obituary published in the *Times* of London stated that Pérez had
provided valuable services to South America and that as director of the influential journal, *Hispania,* he had been forced to
dictate all of his editorials due to being nearly completely
blind. At the start of the war, it continued, "His always vibrant
enthusiasm for the British Empire took a practical form....The
Allies and especially the English owe him a great debt of grat-
itude for his sympathetic efforts and goodwill, and his book
Aspects of the War published in English and Spanish has
reached a vast number of readers."[4]

The last issue of *Hispania* appeared on June 17, 1916. It
featured the photograph reproduced below, and the editorial
team dedicated it to celebrating Pérez Triana's achievements.
The opening article reviewed key points in his career. It concluded that "Colombia had no other defender more brilliant,
more convinced, or more selfless."[5]

Tributes written by his friends and associates: James Fitzmaurice-Kelly, R. B. Cunninghame Graham, Ramiro de
Maeztu, Pedro García Morales, James Douglas, Luis
Bonafoux, and A.G. Gardiner followed this statement.[6] "What
the River Said," an excerpt from Pérez's *De Bogotá al Atlántico,* completed the homage.

In 1915 the Real Academia Española admitted Pérez Triana
and Eduardo Zuleta, an Antioqueñan doctor, novelist and
diplomat, as corresponding members. At the suggestion of this

august academic body, the Academia Colombiana de Lengua also invited both men to become members, but Pérez Triana died before he could accept this honor.[7] At his induction on August 6, 1919 Zuleta read an "Elogía" in memory of Pérez Triana emphasizing that he was a "genuine champion" of Colombia.[8]

Alejandro Álvarez, the editor of *The Monroe Doctrine: Its importance in the International Life of the States of the New World* published in 1924, recognized Pérez Triana's contributions in the effort to Latinize the Monroe Doctrine. This volume contains a documentary history of the doctrine from its inception until 1924 and a compilation of the varying views expressed about the policy by more that 40 Latin American and U.S. statesmen and publicists. In the second section Alvarez included three essays by Pérez Triana: "Wanted: A Revised and Extended Monroe Doctrine," "Origin and Significance of the Monroe Doctrine," and "an American Union."[9]

In Colombia, however, Zuleta's elegy appears to be the last public recognition of Santiago Pérez Triana to this day. If it were not for the literary sketches of his life contained in the published reminisces of his closest colleagues—Luis Eduardo Nieto Caballero and Baldomiro Sanín Cano—and Sergio Elías Ortiz's brief biography, twenty-first century Colombians would find little to remind them of the man who so boldly supported the Drago Doctrine, represented the rights of Latin Americans at the Pan-American Financial Conference in 1915, and called for the Pan-Americanization of the Monroe Doctrine. Suggested below are two possible explanations as to why historians have tended to overlook his role in early twentieth century Colombian history: the first addresses his status as a man of letters and the second his significance as a crusader for hemispheric unity.

The cultural explanation that focuses on Pérez Triana's lack of prestige in Colombia as a man of letters takes inspiration from Cedric Watts' analysis of the career of Pérez Triana's good friend, R. B. Cunninghame Graham. In his summing up of Graham's status in the British literary world, Watts observes that there is a class of writers who fall into the category of "notable has-beens:" "In their day these writers were famous or prestigious; subsequently they have become neglected and forgotten; and from time to time attempts are made by commentators to revive their reputations, but the authors resist revival; they simply have not been good enough to last, it seems. R.B. Cunninghame Graham may be one of these..."[10] Pérez Triana also seems to fit into this category for while he was extremely well-known during his lifetime, since his death in 1916 his work and contributions as a member of the Classic Generation in Colombian history were simply not "good enough to last."

In many ways Pérez shared the attributes of the group of leaders that led Colombia between 1880 and 1905. He was well informed about events in Europe. He read the works of social theorists, studied for three years in Germany, and looked to England as the leader of the Western World. Philosophically, he was deeply committed to the Radical Liberal viewpoint, he had a sentimental attachment to Spanish culture, and he adopted an individualistic, egocentric approach to life.

Yet in other ways he was unique among his contemporaries. Although his Colombian family ties were important to him, he married a North American woman whose inheritance on the death of his father-in-law gave him the means to live abroad in a most luxurious style. He was not particularly interested in teaching and never completed the work to receive a law degree. After 1893 he was not actively engaged in the bitter struggle between Liberals and Conservatives which cumulated in the War of the Thousand Days. His extraordinary facility in mastering languages contributed to his interest in international affairs. It was only in 1903, when the United States brazenly supported the separation of Panama from Colombia that he found his forte in defending in letters, speeches, and written essays the rights of Latin American countries against the threat of European and U.S. imperialism.

Notwithstanding these achievements, even his closest colleagues were quick to point out his shortcomings. Despite all his efforts to dispel their misgivings, many found it difficult to ignore the dark cloud that hung over his commercial dealings in New York City. Moreover, the scandal that surrounded his efforts to produce a railroad contract in Antioquia remained unresolved, and after he fled the country via the Orinoco River in 1893, Pérez Triana knew that he could never return without facing criminal charges of malfeasance.

In an era that valued literary achievements, the works of Pérez Triana failed to reach the high standards set by contemporaries such as Jorge Isaacs (1837–95), José Asunción Silva (1865–96), and Rafael Núñez (1815–94), or even those of his father, Santiago Pérez de Manosalbas. The obituary published in *El Tiempo* stated that although his narratives of his days in Germany and of his travels down the Orinoco were "original and authentic," his literary work was "the weakest part of his intellectual output."[11] Hernando Salazar appears to confirm this assessment for in his anthology, *Parnaso colombiano,* a collection of the poems of 78 Colombian writers, he included only one by Pérez Triana, "Vientos del Llanos." This inclusion came with the added notation that no comprehensive volume of his poetic works had been published.[12] *El Tiempo* also found fault with Pérez Tirana's speeches, describing them as "pompous harangues (*arengas*) lacking the perfection, the greatness of thought or the elegant restraint of the oration his father made over the tomb of Murillo."[13]

It might be argued that Pérez Triana's political writings had

greater resonance in Europe and the United States than in
Colombia. Tomás O. Eastman actually described him as an
"English writer." He stated that Pérez enjoyed great fame as
an English orator, and that the most serious English and North
American newspapers solicited and paid him generously for
his collaboration.[14] Despite this international recognition, the
determination that Pérez Triana's literary works failed to rise
to the standards set by his Colombian colleagues and even by
his father was echoed by Zuleta's eulogy who offered a pithy
comparison of the two Santiagos in his "Elogía." He wrote that
Pérez de Manosalbas had "a precise, sober and mature style of
a true thinker" while Pérez Triana stood out more for his ora-
tory talent. Pérez de Manosalbas was an editor of the quiet
phrase and deep, discrete thought while his son wrote in fluent,
abundant phrases. The father was modest, austere and severe,
while his son "lived when he could in splendor and magnifi-
cence. The one had at his center the struggle of the country;
the other shown under the broad canopy of all the heavens."[15]

   If later generations found fault with Pérez Triana's numerous speeches, these same "pompous harangues" captivated his
contemporary listeners who were amazed at his ability to speak
correctly in five languages and to present his talks entirely
from memory due to his blindness. In fact, his most memorable
attribute was his charismatic personality. As Graham recalled,
"His soul appeared especially modeled for friendship."[16] *El
Tiempo's* obituary conceded that those who knew Pérez would
never forget him for he was what the French call *un charmeur*:
he received with open arms any compatriot that knocked at his
door, and for all he had a gallant phrase or delicate attention.
Many who came with misgivings against him, left after an hour
of talk conquered by that admirable talent that was never as
great or as seductive as in the hours of intimacy when there
came from his lips: "In a dazzling cascade, the most brilliant

phrases, fascinating anecdotes of the present and past, literary reminiscences, poems cited with infallible memory and in perfect circumstances, original and daring judgments about humanity and things, in all a generous and sympathetic conception of life, freely appreciated through a temperament admirably adapted to embrace it fully."[17]

In summing up the life of R. B. Cunninghame Graham, Watts concluded, "His masterpiece, as his contemporaries recognized, was *himself* [emphasis mine], in all his vividness and paradoxical variety."[18] Likewise Pérez Triana's masterpiece was *himself*—a unique personality composed of special qualities easily discounted in the passing of years but faithfully portrayed for all eternity by José Avellanos, the fictional character that Joseph Conrad based on Pérez Triana in *Nostromo*.

If in cultural terms the quality of Pérez Triana's literary essays, books and poems relegate him to the rank of "notable has-beens," Colombian historians have likewise downplayed his contributions as a crusader for hemispheric unity. To offer just one example, in the standard reference work, *Historia diplomática de Colombia 1810–1934*, Raimundo Rivas makes only two references to Pérez Triana. The first discusses his claim to be an American citizen in 1893; the second mentions that he was a delegate to The Hague Convention of 1907 but omits any commentary about his support of the Drago Doctrine at that meeting.[19] Rivas' failure to describe his services to Colombia's diplomatic history as minister plenipotentiary to London and Madrid or his activities as a delegate at the Pan-American Financial Conference appears to be a gross oversight.

James Henderson, who has written extensively on Colombian history in the first half of the twentieth century, has suggested one explanation for this failure to give Pérez Triana his due as a worthy representative of Colombia in international diplomacy. After completing an analysis of the Colombian Congress between 1910 and 1930, he was struck by the enormous difference in the nature of this legislative body between 1910–20 and 1920–30, despite the fact that Conservatives dominated throughout the entire era. In the earlier decade, Congress "retained the nineteenth-century atmosphere of a club composed of wealthy men who regarded the poorer classes, when they thought of them at all, with disdain."[20] Laborers in Colombia were not effectively organized and did not make significant demands for improvements in their working conditions until the aftermath of the Great War. Since Colombia maintained steadfast neutrality in that conflict, only recently have historians begun to study its immense impact on the domestic and foreign affairs of the country. There is, however, some agreement that the conditions it created combined with the effects of the Mexican Revolution (1910–17) and the Bolshevik Revolution of 1917 signaled the end of the status quo, and that the makeup of Congress from 1920–30 reflected this changing Colombian reality.[21]

After the war's conclusion, the long-awaited ratification of the Thomson-Urrutia Treaty in 1921 brought to the country a bonanza of $25 million. This influx of money ushered in the era known as "The Dance of the Millions." During the administrations of President Pedro Nel Ospina (1922–26) and President Miguel Abadía Méndez (1926–30), Colombia moved squarely into the U.S. trade orbit. Not only did coffee find a booming market in the States, but revenues from petroleum and banana exports by U.S. companies brought the government an additional 34 million pesos in 1918. The influx of foreign capital, together with the revival of world markets pulled Colombia out of the economic doldrums and opened an age of unparalleled material progress.[22]

The downside of this bonanza was growing discontent among laborers. The benefits of the economic boom did not filter down to the masses. Mining concessions in gold, platinum, and oil did not help the average Colombian. Very little capital went into the production of foodstuffs and raw materials. Public works programs were supported by miserably low salaries for laborers, and by pulling workers away from agriculture, the programs tended to reduce food production and thus raise living costs. Drawing upon their earlier experiences, workers carried out 83 strikes in the 1920s—a struggle that cumulated in the bloody United Fruit Company strike in 1928.

As a result of these changes, the 1920s saw the development of a militant labor movement that was able to elect to Congress more radical representatives including Jorge Gaitán, Alberto López, and Enrique Olaya Herrera who took up the cause of the workers. Henderson argues that because of their embrace of new ideologies and understanding of Colombia's changing situation in the 1920s, the men belonging to "Los Nuevos" or the "Revolutionary Generation" as they were called, rejected the earlier Classic Generation and follow-on Centenarian Generation of Colombian leaders "root and branch" and having little patience with their low opinion of the Colombian masses.[23]

For the men of this new generation, contributions in the traditional fields of letters and diplomacy accounted for very little. In Pérez Triana's case, they conveniently overlooked that in 1909 he had been a forward-looking nationalist who played a role in the uprising that toppled Rafael Reyes in 1909, and that he fervently condemned the United States for its support of the Panamanian Revolution.

From his base in London, Pérez wrote a constant stream of editorials in *Hispania* that embraced a wider concern of the position of Latin American vis-à-vis Europe. He was a strong supporter of hemispheric solidarity and called for the reworking of the Monroe Doctrine to include Latin America as an equal partner. However, his death in 1916 prematurely re-

moved him from both international and domestic developments that occurred after the end of the Great War. Whether
he would have sympathized with the leaders who made up *Los
Nuevos* can never be known, but Henderson would argue that
his career and achievements belong to that of an earlier age.[24]

In many ways Pérez Triana's base in London was a decided
asset in his work for Colombian interests. As an ex-pat he had
the luxury of distance from the day-to-day political machina-
tions going on in Bogotá. His home served as a rallying point
for others driven from their homelands for political reasons
and provided access to the most notable European thinkers of
his time. From London he could candidly offer his views of
the *Quinquenio* and the Republican Union Party. He could call
for solidarity of all Latin American nations with the United
States without fear of reprisal, and during the Great War his
speeches and publications in stalwart support of the Allies benefitted the United States and Great Britain far more than neutral Colombia.

While Colombians seem to agree that history will remember
Pérez Triana primarily as what the French call a *causeur* (chat-
terer), this designation obscures what was undoubtedly his
greatest contributions to Colombia and Latin America as a
whole. Pérez fervently supported the Drago Doctrine in 1907.
His speeches at the Pan-American Financial Conference and
his publications in pamphlets and newspapers found a recep-
tive audience throughout Europe and the United States as well
as Colombia. In sum, Santiago Pérez Triana was far more than
just a striking, unique personality. He was a crusader who
played a fundamental role in promoting the Latin-American-
ization of the Monroe Doctrine, cultivating support for the Allied cause in the Great War, and building hemispheric unity.

Notes

Preface

1. "Introducción" to Pérez Triana, "De la vera del camino," *Suplemento Literario de El Tiempo*, No. 15, Serie 11 (1914), 65
2. Sergio Elías Ortiz, *Santiago Pérez Triana* (Bogotá: Editorial Kelly, 1971).
3. Ramón Illán Bacca, "Hallazgos," *El Heraldo,* June 8, 2014.
4. Santiago Pérez Triana, *Down the Orinoco in a Canoe* (New York: Thomas Y. Crowell, 1902).
5. Santiago Pérez Triana, *De Bogotá al Atlántico por la via de los ríos Meta, Vichada y Orinoco* (Madrid: Rev. de Archivos, 1905). R. B. Cunninghame Graham, a good friend of Pérez Tirana, wrote the "Introduction" to the English edition while Rubén Darío provided the "Introducción" for the Spanish edition.
6. Baldomero Sanín Cano, "Santiago Pérez Triana," in *Hombres he conocido."* Reprinted in *Escritos* (Bogotá: Editorial Andes, 1977), 742.

Chapter 1

1. Miguel Urrutia M. and Mario Arrubla, ed. *Compendio de estadísticas históricas de Colombia* (Bogotá D. E., National University of Colombia, 1970), 15; Jane M. Rausch, *The Llanos Frontier in Colombian History 1830–1930* (Albuquerque: University of New Mexico Press, 1993), 2.
2. Frank Safford, *The Ideal of the Practical: Colombia's Struggle to Form a Technical Elite* (Austin: University of Texas, 1975), 25.
3. *El Tiempo*, November 30, 1913 cited by Jorge Villegas and José Yunis, eds., *1900–1924 Sucesos Colombianos* (Medellín: Universidad de Antioquia, 1976). (Hereafter cited as SUCESOS), 179.

4. James Park, *Rafael Núñez and the Politics of Colombian Regionalism, 1863–1886* (Baton Rouge: Louisiana State University, 1985), 189.

5. Helen Delpar, *Red against Blue: The Liberal Party in Colombian Politics, 1863–1899* (Tuscaloosa: University: University of Alabama, 1981), 158.

6. On October 18, 1900, an editorial in the Bogotá periodical *La Opinión* marked the first anniversary of the war, stating with wry humor: "In one century we have suffered three international wars, fourteen general revolutions and ten partial revolutions and 300,000 Colombians have died. Unfortunately, our national sport is war, just as England has horses and Spain bull fights." In SUCESOS, 50.

7. Charles Bergquist, *Coffee and Conflict in Colombia* (Durham: Duke University Press, 1978), 242–46.

8. Abel Naranjo Villegas, *Generaciones colombianos* (Bogotá: El Dorado, 1976).

9. Ibid., 73. The other generations Naranjo Villegas classified by birth date were: Heroic (1800–30); Costumbrista (1820–30); Classic (1835–65); Republican (1865–80); Modernist (1880–1910), and Socialistic (1910–40). Since Santiago Pérez de Manosalbas was born in 1830, Naranjo Villegas assigned him to the Costumbrista Generation.

10. James D. Henderson, *Modernization in Colombia: The Laureano Gómez Years, 1889–1965* (Gainesville: University Press of Florida, 2001), 25–27.

11. Delpar, *Red against Blue*, 55.

12. Ibid.

13. Sergio Elías Ortiz, *Santiago Pérez Triana* (Bogotá: Editorial Kelly, 1971), 5.

14. In contrast to Felipe and Santiago, the archives yield little information concerning the youngest brother, Rafael. A search of AncestryLibrary.com reveals that he married Dolores García and that their union produced one daughter, Elivira Pérez, but not even the year of his death has been recorded. See "Rafael Pérez Manosalbas," www.AncestryLibrary.com accessed August 16, 2016.

15. Delpar, *Red against Blue*, 48.

16. Ortiz, *Santiago Pérez Triana*, 6. After completing a brilliant career as writer, politician and journalist, Felipe died at the relatively young age of 55 after being struck down by a horse-drawn carriage in Bogotá on Feb. 26, 1891. See Enrique Pérez, *Vida de*

Felipe Pérez (Bogotá: Impr. De "La Luz," 1911), 5.

17. See Santiago Díaz Piedrahita, *José Jerónimo Triana: naturalista multifacético.* (Bogotá: Fondo Fen Colombia, 1996).
18. Lucela Gómez Giraldo, "Santiago Pérez Manosalbas," *Biografías Biblioteca Virtual del Banco de la República.* For a recent comprehensive study of the Chorographic Commission see Nancy P. Appelbaum, *Mapping the Country of Regions: The Chorographic Commission of Nineteenth-Century Colombia* (Chapel Hill: University of North Carolina Press, 2016).
19. Javier Ocampo López, "Centenario de Santiago Pérez: El presidente, educador y el humanista de la colombianidad," *Revista Credencial Historia* (June 2000) no. 126; Nemesiano Rincón, "Santiago Pérez Triana," in *Desde la cumbre: estudios biográficos* (Quito: Escuela Tipográfica Salesiana, 1940), 59.
20. With the exception of Santiago Pérez Triana, information about his siblings is scanty. Paulina eventually moved to Germany where she married a German identified as "Herr Essen." She died in 1880, apparently with no offspring. Eduardo, however, followed his father into politics. Like Santiago he married an American woman, Janette Swanson and they had at least one child, a daughter, Virginia. In 1905 he was serving as chargé d' affaires of the Colombian Legation in Washington where in spite of the strained relations between the United States and Colombia over the seizure of Panama, he was well received. In October 1905, Eduardo and Janette were transferred to Paris where he had been appointed first Secretary of the Colombian legation. See *Washington Times,* November 5, 1905 and New *York Tribune,* October 21, 1906.
21. Ortiz, *Santiago Pérez Triana,* 8.
22. Ocampo López, "Centenario."
23. From here on to distinguish between the two Santiagos, I will refer to the father as Pérez de Manosalbas and the son as Pérez Triana.
24. Hernando Tellez, "Prologue" to *De Bogotá al Atlántico* (Bogotá: Editorial Kelly, 1942), n.p.
25. Baldomero Sanín Cano, "Santiago Pérez Triana," in *Escritos* (Bogotá: Editorial Andes, 1977), 741.
26. Delpar, *Red against Blue,* 100; Antonio Pérez Aguirre, *25 años de historia Colombiana, 1853 a 1878, del centralismo a la federación* (Bogotá: Editorial Sucre, 1959), 332. In *El olimpo radical* (Bogotá: Talleres Editoriales de Librería Voluntad, 1950), Eduardo Rodríguez Piñeres adds that Pérez de Manosalbas was

president in an age that celebrated irreligiosity and anticlerical-ism, yet he clung to his beliefs as a fervent and convinced Catholic. After he was elected, "he was nicknamed 'El Presidente del librito' because of his habit of going to mass with a prayer book in this hand." (p. 217)

27. Santiago Pérez, "Discurso," in Hernán Valencia Benavides, *Discursos y mensajes de posesión presidencial* (Bogotá: Imprenta Nacional, 1981), I: 147–52.

28. Ibid., 354.

29. Pérez Aguirre, *25 años de historia Colombiana*, 332.

30. Lisa Fetheringill Zwicker. *Dueling Students: Conflict, Masculinity, and Politics in German Universities, 1890–1914* (Ann Arbor: University of Michigan Press, 2011), 18.

31. Ibid., 19–20.

32. Santiago Pérez Triana, *Reminiscencias tudescas* (Madrid: Libr. De Fernando Fe, 1902), 40; "Sketches of Germany," *New Orleans Times*, April 15, 1975, XII, 6545.

33. Ortiz, *Santiago Pérez Triana*, 11.

34. Pérez Triana, *Reminiscencias tudescas*.

35. Ibid., 107–28.

36. Ibid., 59–80.

37. Ibid., 43.

38. Ibid., 81–106. The Corps were the most prestigious of the fraternities tracing their linage directly to the earliest associations students had formed and attracting a large contingency of the aristocracy. Second in status was the Burschenschafts, whose members took pride in their history of nationalist activism from the early nineteenth century. Verbindungs were looser associations. See Zwicker, *Dueling Students,* 29–35.

39. Pérez Triana, *Reminiscencias tudescas*, 62.

40. Ibid., 66–67.

41. Ibid., 138.

42. Ibid., 149.

43. Ibid., 156–57.

44. Eduardo Nieto Caballero, "Prologue," *Reminiscencias*, 31.

45. James Fitzmaurice-Kelly, "Santiago Pérez Triana," in *Hispania* V:54 (June 27, 1916), 1,615.

Chapter 2

1. Santiago Pérez Triana, *Down the Orinoco in a Canoe* (New York: Thomas Crowell, 1902.)
2. Pérez Triana was the only partner in residence in the United States. The other partners lived in Colombia.
3. Marco Palacios, *Between Legitimacy and Violence: A History of Colombia, 1875–2002* (Durham, NC: Duke University Press, 2007), 26.
4. Ibid., 27.
5. Ortiz, *Santiago Pérez Triana*, 20. In an interview with the *New York Tribune* published by the *Chicago Daily Tribune* on April 8, 1885, Pérez Triana supplied details concerning the revolt within Colombia. He estimated that the rebels within the county had a force of some 8,000 to 10,000 men but were woefully short of arms. While there was little doubt that the government had the advantage, he predicted that the struggle would be long and bitter, and he added that with few exceptions Colombian merchants in New York City were Liberals who sympathized with the rebels.
6. Ibid., 22.
7. Ibid., 23–26. Later Pérez Triana published two pamphlets, *Una explicación* (New York, 1887) and *De política y mercantile* (New York, 1887) to explain and defend the activities of Pérez Triana y Compañía in this matter.
8. Eduardo Zuleta, "Elogio de Don Santiago Pérez Triana" (Read in the Academia Colombiana de la Lengua on August 6, 1919 and published in *Anuario de la Academia Colombiana de la Lengua* (Bogotá, 1937) IV: 242–55.
9. Ibid., 391. Juan Antonio Pérez Bonalde (1846–92) was a Venezuelan romantic poet and translator who lived many years in exile. Of his numerous translations of English, German, Italian and French writers into Spanish, his translation of *The Raven* by Edgar Allan Poe published in 1887 is one of his best known.
10. U.S. Passport application, 1795–1925, http://interactive.ancestrylibrary.com accessed August 16, 2016. Pérez's passport describes him as a man, 31 years of age, 5'5 ½" tall, with a full face, high forehead, dark brown eyes, a broad nose, full mouth, black hair and chin, and a dark complexion.
11. *New York Times,* May 27, 1890. On October 14, 1894 the *St Louis Post-Dispatch* under the headline "A High Indebtedness," stated that when Pérez Triana left New York City in 1890, his affairs

were in such a tangled state that "after four years of hard work neither the lawyers nor anyone else can tell how much he owes. It is certain that his indebtedness runs very high." www.newspapers.com/image/138162627 accessed August 16, 2016.

12. Baldomero Sanín Cano, "Santiago Pérez Triana," *Escritos* (Bogotá: Editorial Andes, 1977), 745.

13. Santiago Pérez Triana, *La Casa de Pérez Triana & Cia a Sus Relacionados* (Medellín: Imprenta de El Espectador, 1890).

14. Ibid., 15–16. His unresolved legal status made it impossible for him to consider returning to the United States where he would face legal charges.

15. Ibid., 746.

16. Juan Santiago Correa Restrepo, "El ferrocarril de Antioquia: empresarios extranjeros y participación local," *Estudios gerenciales* 28:123 (April–June 2012), 5. For more information about Cisneros' experience in Colombia, see Hernán Horna, "Los ferrocarriles latinoamericanos del siglo XIX: el caso Colombia," in Carlos Dávila and L. de Guevara, *Empresas y empresarios en la historia de Colombia. Siglos XIX–XX: Una colección de estudios recientes* (Bogotá: Norma, 2003), II: 1021-1044.

17. As a result of the adoption of the Constitution of 1886 the national regions formerly known as states were renamed departments.

18. Juan Santiago Correa Restrepo, "El ferrocarril de Antioquia: empresarios extranjeros y participación local," ED Estudios Gerenciales, 28:123 (April–June 2012). http://www.icesi.edu.co/ revistas/index.php/estudiosgerenciales/article/view/1213/html accessed December 15, 2015.

19. La Quiebra is a formidable peak in the Cordillera Occidental that posed a seemingly insurmountable barrier to the completion of the railroad. The problem was not solved until 1929 when a decision was made to construct a tunnel of more than 3,500 meters through the mountain. See Alberto Mayor Mora, "Túnel de La Quiebra," *Revista Credencial Historia*, (Agosto 1999), No. 1116.

20. Correa Restrepo makes clear that the decision to involve Pérez Triana in the negotiations was an "error" with "the worst possible results." See his *Los caminos de hierro* (Bogotá: CESA, Comunicaciones, 2010), 64.

21. Ortiz, *Santiago Pérez Triana*, 35–37.

22. Ibid., 38.

23. Correa Restrepo, "El Ferrocarril."

24. Ibid.; Ortiz, *Santiago Pérez Triana*, 40.

25. Sanín Cano, "Santiago Pérez Triana," 736–37.

26. Delpar, *Red against Blue*, 154–55.

27. Pérez Triana to John T. Abbott, April 19, 1893. U.S. Department of State Dispatches from U.S. Ministers in Colombia, Microcopy Roll 50, February 1–July 17, 1893. (Hereafter cited as Dispatches.)

28. Letter from Minister of War to Santiago Pérez Triana, April 22, 1893. Dispatches.

29. Sanín Cano, "Santiago Pérez Triana," 739.

30. Telegram, Henry Hallam to L.F. McKinney, Honda, September 16, 1893. Dispatches.

31. Luther McKinney to Walter Q. Gresham, Secretary of State, Washington D.C., January 12, 1894. Dispatches.

32. Sanin Cano, "Santiago Pérez Triana, 740.

33. Ibid., 740, 746; Ortiz, *Santiago Pérez Triana,* 50–67.

34. The travelers exchanged their horses for mules because mules, being more patient and sure-footed beasts of burden, were a better choice for the long journey ahead.

35. Santiago Pérez Triana, *Down the Orinoco in a* Canoe (New York: Crowell, 1902), 47. Subsequent direct quotations will be taken from this edition.

36. Ibid., 55.

37. Ibid., 76.

38. Ibid., 89.

39. Ibid.

40. The Meta, the Vichada, and the Orinoco form a triangle of which the last named is the base. The Vichada enters the main stream some fifty miles above, and the Meta about 200 miles below. Ibid., 116.

41. Ibid., 120.

42. Tonka beans were an export product used in Europe as a substitute for vanilla extract.

43. Ibid., 213.

Chapter 3

1. Delpar, *Red against Blue,* 158; Deas, "Colombia, Ecuador and Venezuela, c. 1880–1930." In *Cambridge History of Latin America,* 5 vols. (Cambridge, 1984–86), V: 647.

2. In 1891 for example, he published a poem "Otoño" in *La Revista Ilustrada de Nueva York* (no. 11 de 1891). See Rincón, "Santiago Pérez Triana," 78.

3. Santiago Pérez Triana, *El deber de cantar: cantos colombianos* (Lausana: Imprenta Jorge Bridal, 1899).

4. A. J. Restrepo, "Por el Poeta," in Santiago Pérez Triana, *El deber de cantar,* 15.

5. Ibid., 39–40. English translations are by the author. Pérez Triana dedicated the other poems in this collection to Fidel Cano, Eustario de la Torre Narvaez, Rafael Salcedo Campo, J. de D. Uribe, J. B. Echeverría, and Rafael Uribe Uribe.

6. *El Nuevo Tiempo Literario* republished "A una desconocida" on October 4, 1908 in Vol. VII: 9–2128. It is reprinted and translated in the Appendix.

7. UK, Incoming Passenger Lists, 1878–1960, www.AncestryLibrary.com accessed August 18, 2016.

8. Ortiz, *Santiago Pérez Triana*, 73; Nieto Caballero in his "Prologue," *Reminiscencias,* 8–9 suggests that they may have met in New York City, but Plata's account appears to be more plausible.

9. O'Day was a close personal friend of John D. Rockefeller, and as the mastermind of oil transportation, he was one of the five original oil men who organized the Standard Oil Co. He was also president of the People's Bank of Buffalo and on the board of directors of many important companies. In 1902 he built a magnificent Tudor mansion on 85 acres along Deal Lake in Monmouth County, New Jersey. When the estate was completed, he hosted a grand party for 2,000 guests on June 22, 1903. http://www.hometoclare.com/clarepeople/daniel-oday accessed August 18, 2016.

10. This account is recorded both by Ortiz, *Santiago Pérez Triana,* p. 74 and Nieto Caballero, *Reminiscencias,* 8–9.

11. http://interactive.ancestrylibrary.com accessed August 18, 2016.

12. L. E. Nieto Caballero, "Santiago Pérez Triana," in *Hombres del Pasado* (Bogotá: Ediciones Terra Firma, 1944), 20.

13. "Santiago Pérez Triana," *Hispania* V:54 (June 27, 1916), 1.

14. Cedric Watts, *R. B. Cunninghame Graham* (Boston: Twayne Publishers, 1983), 1–19.

15. "Robert Bontine Cunninghame Graham," https://en.wikipedia.org/wiki/Robert_Bontine_Cunninghame_Graham accessed June 24, 2016.

16. Baldomiro Sanín Cano, *De mi vida y otras vidas* (Bogotá: Editorial ABC, 1949), 89–90.

17. Cedric Watts and Laurence Davies, *Cunninghame Graham: A Critical Biography* (Cambridge: Cambridge University Press, 1979), 217.

18. Ibid., 114. The similarities with Pérez Triana are clear as soon as Conrad first introduces Don José Avellanos in Chapter 5 of *Nostromo:* "Don José Avellanos, their neighbour across the street, a statesman, a poet, a man of culture who had represented his country at several European courts (and had suffered untold indignities as a state prisoner in the time of the tyrant Guzman Bento), used to declare in Doña Emilia's drawing room that Carlos had all the English qualities of character with a truly patriotic heart." When Don José Avellanos visited Doña Emilia, he would take tea and "talk on and on with a sort of complacent virtuosity wonderful in a man of his age while he held the cup in his hands for a long time." See Joseph Conrad, *Nostromo* (1904) (New York: Doubleday, 1960), 54.

19. Malcolm Deas, "Joseph Conrad: Nostromo y Colombia," *Credencial Historia,* Edición 35 (Nov. 1992).

20. Nieto Caballero, "Santiago Pérez Triana,"34.

21. Peregrinación a la Tumba de Santiago Pérez, 23 May 1911 (Paris: Librería Paul Ollendorff, 1911), 25–28.

22. Ortiz, *Santiago Pérez Triana,* 75–76.

23. Zuleta, Elogía, 394–95.

24. Sanín Cano, 748; Ortiz, 81. I am using the term *"revista"* here to refer to a journal that might include news, literary criticism, and political essays.

25. Cited by Ortiz, *Santiago Pérez Triana,* 84. Diplomat, writer, critic, and author of *Pepita Jiménez* (1874), Juan Valera was one of the most influential Spanish intellectuals at the turn of the nineteenth century.

26. R. B. Cunninghame Graham, "Introduction," in *Down of the Orinoco in a Canoe* (New York: Thomas Crowell, 1902), vii–x.

27. The 20 reviews translated into Spanish were reprinted in the second Spanish edition of the book, that also included a preface by Rubén Darío and was published in Madrid in 1905. The *Daily Chronicle* review can be found on pp. 349–51.

28. *New York Times,* May 16, 1903.

29. Others included Hiram Bingham, *Journal of an Expedition across Venezuela and Colombia* (New Haven: Yale, 1909); Miguel Triana, *Al Meta* (Bogotá: Casa Editorial El Liberal, 1913); and H. J. Mozans, *Up the Orinoco and down the Magdalena* (New York: D. Appleton, 1910).

30. Miguel Triana, *Por el sur de Colombia* (Paris: Garnier Hermanos, 1907).

31. Pérez Triana, "Prólogo," in Miguel Triana, *Por el sur de Colombia,* xxiii.

32. Santiago Pérez Triana, *Tales to Sonny* (London: Anthony Threherne & Co., 1906).
33. Pérez Triana, "Prefacio," *Cuentos a Sonny* (Madrid: Imprenta y Estereotipia de Ricardo Fé, 1907), 25–26.
34. Tomás O. Eastman, "Prólogo," Pérez Triana, *Cuentos a Sonny*, 12–15.
35. Nieto Caballero, "Santiago Pérez Triana," *Reminiscencias*, 12–14.
36. "Standard Oil's Traffic Pioneer, O'Day, is Dead," *New York Times,* September 14, 1906.
37. L. C. Nieto Caballero, "Santiago Pérez Triana," *Hombres del pasado* (Bogotá: Ediciones "Tierra Firme" Litografía Colombia, 1944), 19–21.

Chapter 4

1. Sanín Cano, "Santiago Pérez Triana," 737.
2. Between 1905 and 1914 Pérez Triana corresponded regularly with his cousin, Diego Mendoza Pérez whose mother was the sister of Santiago Pérez de Manosalbas. Fifty-two of these letters survive in the BLAA and provide some insight into his more intimate thoughts. In addition, the BLAA has an archive of 13 letters that he wrote to his nephew, Jorge Lagos M. between 1908 and 1911.
3. The French Canal Company founded in 1879 initiated work on building a canal through Panama in 1883 but was declared bankrupt in 1888 because of scandals concerning its management. In 1890 thanks to the efforts of deLesseps, the firm was reorganized and later granted an extension until 1910, but it was never able to complete construction as planned. After 1902 it sold most of its assets to the United States. See Robert H. Davis, *Historical Dictionary of Colombia* 2nd ed. (Metuchen, N. J.: The Scarecrow Press, 1993), 152.
4. Jane M. Rausch, *The Llanos Frontier in Colombian History 1830–1930* (Albuquerque: University of New Mexico Press, 1993), 204.
5. Bergquist offers a good but brief survey of the Reyes years in *Coffee and Conflict,* 224–46.
6. Jesús María Henao and Gerardo Arrubla, *Historia de Colombia,* (Bogotá: Camacho Roldán, 1929), 765.
7. Darío Mesa, "La vida política después de Panamá." In *Manual*

de historia de Colombia (Bogotá: Instituto Colombiano de Cultura, 1978–80), 96.

8. BLAA. Santiago Pérez Triana to Diego Mendoza, London, March 6, 1908.

9. Santiago Pérez Triana *Desde lejos (asuntos colombianos)* (London: Wertheimer, Lea & Co, 1907).

10. Ibid., xix.

11. Bergquist, *Coffee and Conflict*, 234–34.

12. Abel Cruz Santos, "Economía y Hacienda Pública. De la República unitaria a la economía del medio siglo." *Historia Extensa de Colombia* (Vol XV: T. 2 Bogotá: Editorial Lerner, 1966), 115.

13. Jorge Holguín, *Desde cerca* (Paris, 1908) Chapter X, "La Pizarra," 71–75.

14. Pérez Triana, *Desde lejos*

15. Jorge Holguín, *Desde cerca: asuntos colombianos* (Paris: Librairie Generale et Internationale G. Ficker), 1908.

16. Cruz Santos, "Economía y Hacienda Pública," 115.

17. Santiago Pérez Triana, *Desde lejos y desde cerca: (asuntos colombianos)* (London: Imprenta Wertheimer, 1909).

18. Carta 3 dirigida a su sobrino, Jorge Lagos, February 26, 1909, manuscrito. Biblioteca Luis Angel Arango.

19. Cartas 4 and 5 dirigida a su sobrino, March 4 and March 17, 1909; see also SUCESOS March 1909, p. 118.

20. Ortiz, *Santiago Pérez Triana*, 84.

21. Ibid., 85; Nemesiano Rincón, "Santiago Pérez Triana," 75.

22. Pérez Triana, "Carta al Presidente Taft en pro de la honradez internacional," (London: Wertheimer, Lea & Co., 1909), 4.

23. Ibid., 6.

24. Ibid., 16.

25. W. T. Stead, "Introducción," *La Doctrina Drago: colección de Documentos con una Advertencia Preliminar de S. Pérez Triana y una introducción de W. T. Stead* (London: Wertheimer, Lea & Co, 1908), lxiv. (Hereafter cited as *La Doctrina Drago.*)

26. Juan Manuel Pérez, "Drago Doctrine," *Encyclopedia of Latin American History and Culture* ed. Barbara A. Tenenbaum 5 vols. (New York: Charles Scribner's Sons, 1996), II:405.

27. Ibid.

28. A key source for both Hague conferences is James Brown Scott, *The Hague Peace Conferences of 1899 and 1907* 2 vols. (New York & London: Garland Publishing, 1972.)

29. Ortiz, *Santiago Pérez Triana*, 95.

30. "Declaración del General Porter," *La Doctrina Drago*, 160–62.

31. Pérez Triana, "Discurso," in *La Doctrina Drago,* 113–18.
32. Ortiz, *Santiago Pérez Triana*, 98. This scene is eloquently described by R. B. Cunninghame Graham in *Hispania* V:54 (June 27, 1916), 1618.
33. Scott, *The Hague Peace Conferences of 1899 and 1907*, II: 357.
34. Ibid., II: 529.
35. Raimundo Rivas, *Historia diplomática de Colombia 1810–1934* (Bogotá: Imprenta Nacional, 1961), 651.
36. "Courrier de la Conférence," in *La Doctrina Drago*, 207
37. *The Tribune* (London), July 19, 1907 in *La Doctrina Drago,* 216.
38. Ortiz, *Santiago Pérez Triana*, 99. William Thomas Stead was an English journalist, who was drawn into reform politics in the 1880s. He was most famous in Britain for having successfully promoted the first child-protection law. He authored many books. In 1890, he started a periodical, *The Review of Reviews* to which Pérez Triana would be a frequent contributor.
39. "Personajes del año," *Credencial Historia* (Bogotá) Vol. 175, July 2004. There seems to be a discrepancy in the sources as to whether Pérez Triana presented his speeches in French or English at the Convention, but he was capable of using either language fluently. http://www.banrepculural.org/blaavirtual/revistas/credencial/julio2004/personajes,htm
40. Pérez Triana, "Advertencia Preliminar," *Doctrina Drago*, x.
41. Ibid., xli.
42. Ibid., xlix.
43. Ibid., li.
44. Pérez Triana, "Advertencia Preliminar," *La Doctrina Drago*, liv.
45. Juan Pablo Scarfi, "In the Name of the Americas: The Pan-American Redefinition of the Monroe Doctrine and the Emerging Language of American International Law in the Western Hemisphere, 1898–1933," *Diplomatic History*, 40:2 (April 2016), 204.
46. Ibid., 217.
47. Pérez Triana to Diego Mendoza, September 9, 1908; February 20, 1909.
48. Pérez Triana to Diego Mendoza, May 19, 1909. This news was premature for Reyes did not leave his post as president until June 13.

Chapter 5

1. Rausch, *The Llanos Frontier*, 221.
2. Sanín Cano, "Santiago Pérez Triana," 749.
3. Santiago Pérez Triana, *Eslabones sueltos (asuntos colombianos)* (London: Wertheimer, Lea & Co., 1910), v. In a letter dated July 3, 1909 to Jorge Lagos, Pérez explained that however much he might wish to return to Colombia, the government was publicizing the fact that if he did come back, he would have to face the criminal charges he had avoided when he fled the country in 1893. Moreover, his doctors had diagnosed diabetes which would make such travel very difficult. Both were compelling reasons to justify his unwillingness to represent the city of Manizales. See also, Pérez Triana to Diego Mendoza, May 22, 1909.
4. Gonzalo Cataño, "Mendoza Pérez, Diego," in *Biografías Biblioteca Virtual del Banco de la Republica*. During the next eight years, Mendoza was elected as a Liberal to the Cámara de Representantes, and in 1915 he held the post of Minister of Hacienda.
5. Pérez Triana, *Eslabones sueltos,* xii.; Nieto Caballero, "Santiago Pérez Triana," 30–32.
6. Ibid.
7. Henderson, *Modernization,* 78.
8. Pérez Triana, *Eslabones sueltos,* xxxii, xlvii.
9. Henderson, *Modernization,* 78.
10. Pérez Triana, *Unificación de deudas (asuntos colombianos)* (London: Wertheimer, Lea & Co, 1912), 5–11.
11. Nieto Caballero, "Santiago Pérez Triana," 35. This stroke may have been the second one he experienced for on October 1, 1910 Pérez Triana wrote to Jorge Lagos that he had suffered "un ataque de congestion cerebral." He added that the situation was not grave but would impede his early return to Colombia. See BLAA, Carta #12 Pérez Triana to Jorge Lagos M., October 1, 1910.
12. *The Times* (London), May 29, 1916. https://www.newspapers.com/image/33271110 accessed on September 6, 2016.
13. Sanín Cano, "Santiago Pérez Triana," 749–50.
14. Santiago Pérez Triana, "Hispania," *Hispania* (London) I:1 (January 1, 1912).
15. This unnamed reviewer is cited by Ortiz, *Santiago Pérez Triana,* 110.
16. "Dickens," *Hispania* I:3 (March 1, 1912), 68.
17. *Hispania,* I:5 (May 1, 1912), 132–33.

18. "De la vera del camino" was reprinted in the *Suplemento Literario de El Tiempo* (Vol. 2, 15), 67–78.

19. Norman Angell, *Europe's Optical Illusion* (London: Simkin, Marshall, Hamilton, Kent, 1909). After 1910 *The Great Illusion* was subsequently reprinted in various enlarged and revised editions.

20. J. D. B. Miller, "Norman Angell and Rationality in International Relations," in D. Long and P. Wilson, eds, *Thinkers of the Twenty Years' Crisis.* (Oxford: Clarendon Press, 1995), 105.

21. Angell was an English lecturer, journalist, author and member of Parliament for the Labour Party. By the start of W.W. I, he had returned to England to become one of the founders of the Union of Democratic Control. He was knighted in 1931 for his public service and awarded the Nobel Peace Prize in 1933.

22. Santiago Pérez Triana, "Introducción," in Norman Angell, *La Grande Ilusión* trans. by S. Restrepo (Paris: Thomas Nelson and Sons, 1913), 21–35. He published it earlier as "La Gran Ilusión" in *Hispania* I:1 (January 1, 1912), 1–14, and referred to the book once again in *Hispania* II:23 (November 1, 1913), 800–02.

23. Pérez Triana, "Introducción," 32.

24. Ibid., 35.

25. Both of these essays are reprinted in Santiago Pérez Triana, *The Pan-American Financial Conference of 1915* (London: William Heinemann, 1915). The "Manifest" appears on pp.115–34, and the "Memorandum" is on pp. 135–39. The citations that follow are from the 1915 volume. *The Review of Reviews* was a noted family of monthly journals founded in 1890–93 by William T. Stead.

26. Pérez Triana, "Memorandum," 137.

27. Ibid., 138.

28. Ibid., 139.

29. *Review of Reviews* (London) 45:267 (March 1912), 255–67. Pérez Triana also reprinted the "Manifest" in his *The Pan-American Financial Conference of 1915* and subsequent citations are from this book rather than *Hispania*.

30. W.T. Stead was a career journalist who crusaded for such causes as British-Russian friendship, the reform of England's criminal codes, and the maintenance of international peace. His *Review of Reviews* begun in January 1890 is sometimes regarded as a forerunner of contemporary British tabloids. He authored many books and essays including two that predicted the sinking of the RMS *Titanic*. Ironically, he was among the passengers who died

after the *Titanic* struck an iceberg on April 15, 1912 and was eulogized by Pérez Triana in the May 1, 1912 issue of *Hispania.*

31. Pérez Triana, "Manifest" in *The Pan-American Financial Conference of 1915*, 118.

32. Ibid., 121. During the Italo-Turkish War of 1911–12 Italian forces quickly occupied the towns of Tripoli, Derna and Benghazi, but unexpected resistance on the part of the Muslim population forced them to confine their operations to the coastal areas. The war remained at a stalemate until a successful Italian offensive in North Africa from June to October in 1912 convinced Turkey to sue for peace. By the Treaty of Lausanne, October 18, 1912, Turkey conceded its rights over Tripoli and Cyrenaica to Italy and permitted Italian forces to continue to occupy some of the Dodecanese islands off the Turkish coast.

33. Ibid., 125.

34. Ibid., 128.

35. Ibid., 132.

36. Ibid.

37. *Hispania* I:7 (July 1, 1912), 224–28.

38. *The Times of London*, July 30, 1912. https: www.newspapers.com/image/33247284 accessed on December 30, 2016.

39. *Hispania*, II:7 (July 1, 1913), 19–57.

40. Ibid.

41. Ibid.

42. Palacios, *Between Legitimacy and Violence*, 66–67.

43. Rivas, *Historia diplomática*, 656.

44. Colombian delegates were signatories to this convention, and although it was not ratified by the Colombian Senate, Suárez nevertheless adhered to it.

45. Rausch, *Colombia and World War I*, 34.

46. According to the Porter Convention, when the recourse to arbitration does not succeed, the creditor still maintains the right to intervene and take military actions. See James Brown Scott, *The Hague Peace Conferences of 1899 and 1907*, I: 420.

47. *Hispania* III:11 (November 1, 1914), 1237; *New York Times*, December 13, 1914.

48. Ibid.

49. *New York Times*, "Noted South American Diplomat on Monroe Doctrine of Future," December 13, 1914.

50. Roberto Ancízar was head of the Colombian Legation to the United States.

51. Mexico was a conspicuous absentee. *Proceedings of the First*

Pan American Financial Conference (Washington D.C.: Government Printing Office, 1915), 8.

52. Sanín Cano, "Santiago Pérez Triana," 751.

53. *Hispania* V:54 (June 27, 1915), 1618,

54. Sanín Cano, "Santiago Pérez Triana," 751. According to passport records Gertrude had travelled to New York with Sonny (but without her husband) in 1904 and 1905. In December 1912 she made the crossing in the *Lusitania* accompanied by Sonny, who was now 14 years old, and her maid. In 1915 she travelled to Washington, D.C. with her husband who was accompanied by a trained nurse. See http://www.ancestry.com/inst/discoveries/

55. Santiago Pérez Triana, *The Pan-American Financial Conference of 1915*, (London: William Heinemann, 1915), 5.

56. Ibid.

57. Ibid., "The Trusteeship of Liberty," 45–46.

58. John Bassett Moore, "The Pan-American Financial Conferences and the Inter-American High Commission," *The American Journal of International Law* 14:3 (July 1920), 343–44.

59. *El Tiempo*, May 21, 1915; SUCESOS, 225–26.

60. In October 1915 Pérez Triana published *The Pan-American Financial Conference of 1915* (London: William Heinemann, 1915) which was a collection of his speeches delivered at the conference and during the tour of U.S. cities on which the delegates embarked when it was over. It also included an essay that elaborated his definition of "Pan-Americanism." In a "Preparatory Note" he explained: "The fact that the writing and speeches contained in the following pages were published or delivered at various times and in different places, in the advocacy of the same idea, should explain the recurrence of certain utterances and concepts that will be found in them. The hammer strikes and must strike in wearying identity and repetition, yet it is only thus that the iron yields." (p.3) On June 6, 1915 the *New York Times* published the main portion of "The Inviolability of the Continent" under the headline, "All-America Slogan, 'Hands Off!' Nation of Western Hemisphere should Warn Europe Against Land-Grabbing Here, Says Pérez Triana."

61. Pérez Triana, *The Pan-American Financial Conference*, 47–56; Proceedings, 173–77.

62. Proceedings, 474.

63. Ibid., 475–78; Pérez Triana, *The Pan American Financial Conference*, 62–64,

64. Pérez Triana, *The Pan-American Financial Conference*, 9. Sec-

onding Thomson's evaluation was that of the editor of *Nation's Business* who began an article entitled "Colombia" that was published on June 15, 1915 with the following paragraph: "The most eloquent remarks made in the open session of the Conference by members of the visiting delegations from Latin America were contributed by Mr. Santiago Pérez Triana, head of the Colombian Delegation and formerly Colombian Minister to Great Britain. Mr. Triana is an authority on finance and trade, and in his speech on America for the Americans, practically struck the key note of the Conference." (*Nation's Business* (pre-1986); June 15, 1915; 3, 6; ProQuest Business collection, p. 1116.

65. Pérez Triana, *The Pan-American Financial Conference*, 65–78.

66. Ibid., 79–84.

67. Ibid., 85–91.

68. Ibid.

69. In *The Pan American Financial Conference of 1915*, Pérez Triana states that he gave this speech on June 20, but *The New York Times* on June 13 reported that he presented it on June 12 which given the progress of the delegates' U.S. tour seems a more likely date.

70. Ibid., 99–113.

71. *New York Times*, "Urges a Covenant to Guard Americas," June 13, 1915.

72. *Hispania*, July 1, 1915.

73. *Hispania*, August 1, 1915. Here again Pérez Triana gives the date of the speech as June 20.

74. Pérez Triana, "The Pan-American Financial Conference," in *The Pan-American Financial Conference of 1915*, 5–6.

75. Ibid., 41.

76. Ibid., 46.

77. Pérez Triana, "Pan-Americanism," in *The Pan-American Financial Conference of 1915*, 13–14.

78. Ibid., 22.

79. Ibid., 23.

80. Ibid., 28.

81. Ibid., 31.

82. Ibid., 33.

Chapter 6

1. Nieto Caballero, "Prologue," *Reminiscencias*, 32.
2. *The Times*, September 17, 1914. https://www.newspapers.com/ image/33253049 accessed on September 6, 2016.
3. Marco Fidel Suárez, *Informe de 1915*, V: 483–85.
4. Rausch, *Colombia and World War I*, 27.
5. Cited by James Henderson, *Conservative Thought in Twentieth Century Latin America: The Ideas of Laureano Gómez* (Athens: Ohio University, Monographs in International Studies Latin America Series, No. 13, 1988), 79–80.
6. "Calibán" was the pseudonym of Enrique Santos Montejo (1886–1971), an influential journalist and member of the most progressive sector of the Liberal Party. He founded *La Linterna* in 1909 which existed until 1919.
7. Calibán, "La conflagración europea," in *Danza de las horas y otros escritos* (Bogotá: Editorial Club de Lectores, 1969), 34–37.
8. Sanín Cano, *De mi vida y otras vidas*, 94.
9. Watts and Davies, *Cunninghame Graham*, 240–41.
10. A. F. Tschiffely, *Don Roberto: Being the Account of the Life and Works of Robert Bontine Cunninghame Graham, 1852–1936* (London: William Heinemann, 1937), 363.
11. Watts and Davies, *Cunninghame Graham*, 242.
12. Ortiz also mentioned this incident, but he cites Sanín Cano as his source. In addition, the "rift" between the two men must have happened after February 10, 1916 because Graham invited Pérez Triana to speak on that evening at the National Liberal Club in London and introduced him there in the warmest terms.
13. Pérez Triana, *Some Aspects of the War* (London: T. Fisher Unwin, 1915). He had already published some of the chapters of this book as editorials in *Hispania.*
14. bid., 176. The *New York Times* published this chapter on February 26, 1916 with the headline, "Why a Spanish American should not be Pro-German."
15. Ibid., 11.
16. Ibid., 207–15.
17. *New York Times Book Review* 20:306 (August 29, 1915).
18. Cited in the *Book Review Digest*, 12: 662.
19. *Hispania,* V:54 (June 27, 1916), 1621.
20. On March 17, 1915, the *Times* of London cited his essays in *His-*

pania in support of the Allies as a pleasant corrective to the "flood of mendacious literature with which the Germans are attempting to poison public opinion in Spanish-speaking countries."

21. Statement published in *Gil Blas* on May 25 and republished in *El Tiempo* on May 26, 1916.

22. Santiago Pérez Triana, "The Neutrality of Latin America" in *Hispania*, V:3 (March 1, 1916) 5. Citations here are from a published pamphlet which, in addition to the talk, includes an account of the meeting held by the National Liberal Club of London, an Appendix listing the dates of U.S. recognition of the Spanish American republics; the area and population of the republics, and extensive footnotes supporting statements in his talk. Graham's warm introduction of Pérez appears to refute Sanín Cano's assertion of a rift between the two men. The actual speech was also published in Spanish in the March 1, 1916 issue of *Hispania.*

23. Ibid., 11.

24. Ibid., 18.

25. Ibid., 20.

26. Ibid., 22.

27. Ibid., 29.

28. Ibid., 31.

29. Ibid., 34.

30. bid., 35.

31. Fisher Unwin misstates the date here. Pérez Triana did not attend the first Hague Convention in 1899.

32. Ibid., 37.

33. Ibid.

34. José María Quijano Wallis, *Memorias autobiográficas, historia-políticas y de carácter social de José María Quijano Wallis* (Grottaferrata: Tipografía Italo-Orientale, 1919), 7–8.

35. http://www.ancentry.com/inst/; Email from notifications@ancestry.co.uk to Ingrid Natalia Ortiz Hernandez, May 20, 2016; *New York Times,* May 7, 1919.

36. *New York Herald,* November 21, 1919. Although the influenza epidemic in the United States was winding down by November 1919, Sonny's fatal symptoms present the characteristics of that terrible disease.

Chapter 7

1. *El Tiempo,* May 25, 1916.
2. "Nota sobre Pérez Tirana," El Gráfico Series XXX: VI: 291 (June 3, 1916), 157–60. Following Rodriguez's statement, El Gráfico completed its homage with a photo of Pérez Triana and the inclusion of an excerpt of a study of his career that Nieto Caballero was in the process of writing. That sketch of Pérez Triana's life first appeared in Cultura (Bogotá) 6:32 (November 1918), 65–95 and was reprinted in Hombres del pasado (Bogotá: Ediciones Terra Firma, Litografía Colombia, 1944), 15–35.
3. *New York Times,* May 26, 1916.
4. Reprinted in *Hispania* V:54 (June 27, 1916), 1622.
5. *Hispania* V:54 (June 27, 1916), 1616.
6. Douglas's tribute was also published in *The Star* (London), while that of Bonafoux appeared in *Heraldo* (Madrid) and that of A.G. Gardiner in *Daily News & Leader* (London).
7. The Academia Colombiana de la Lengua was founded in 1871 and was the first official Spanish-language academy to be established outside Spain.
8. Eduardo Zuleta, "Elogía de Santiago Pérez Triana," *Anuario de la Academia Colombiana de la Lengua* (Bogotá, 1937) IV: 242–55.
9. Alejandro Álvarez, *The Monroe Doctrine: Its Importance in the International Life of the States of the New World* (New York: Oxford University Press, 1924). It is interesting to note that Álvarez also included a piece by Pérez's fellow Colombian and nemesis, Rafael Reyes. Originally published in the *New York Times* on September 21, 1913, the article entitled, "Go slow with Latin America–Warns Gen. Reyes," emphasized that "there must be no big stick, and no such use of the Monroe Doctrine as to make it an instrument of terror to the smaller republics and a subject for ridicule in the greater countries of the South." p. 342–44.
10. Watts, *R.B. Cunninghame Graham*, 1.
11. "Santiago Pérez Triana," *El Tiempo*, May 25, 1916.
12. Hernando Salazar, ed. *Parnaso colombiano* (Bogotá: Ediciones "Triangulo," 1975), 373; 531.
13. *El Tiempo*, May 25, 1916; Manuel Murillo Toro was a radical Liberal and president of Colombia, 1864–66 and 1872–74 who died on December 26, 1880.
14. Ospina, *Diccionario Biográfico*, III: 281–82.

15. Zuleta, "Elogía," 401.

16. *Hispania* V:54 (June 27, 1916), 1617–18.

17. *El Tiempo,* May 25, 1916.

18. Watts and Davies, *Cunninghame Graham,* xiii.

19. Rivas, *Historia diplomática,* 540; 650.

20. James Henderson, "El congreso frente a las movilizaciones sociales y obreras, 1910–1930," 26. (A chapter in a forthcoming book by Eduardo Posada Carbó.)

21. See Rausch, *Colombia and World War I,* x.

22. Henderson, *Modernization,* 144–15; Rausch, *Colombia and World War I,* 113.

23. Henderson, "El congreso frente a las movilizaciones sociales," 26.

24. In an email to the author on October 10, 2016, Henderson affirmed that the "young Turks of the radical 1920s political generation…all of a socialist and even Marxist-Leninist mindset not seen previously in Colombia, viewed their elders with disdain." They ruthlessly consigned to the ash can of history the political leaders of Pérez Triana's Classical Generation and those of the Centenarian Generation that succeeded it for failing to bring into the political equations the interests of the masses of ordinary people.

Appendix

1. Hernando Salazar, ed. *Parnaso Colombiano* (Medellín: Carpel Antorcha, n.d.), 531.

2. Ibid., 373–75.

Bibliography

I. Archives

U.S. Department of State Dispatches from United States Minister in Colombia. Washington D. C. 1962. Microcopy T33, roll 50, Feb. 1–July 17, 1893; Roll 51, May 12, 1893–August 25, 1894.

II. Primary Sources: Writings of Santiago Pérez Triana including Books, Pamphlets, and Letters

"Advertencia Preliminar" in *La Doctrina Drago: colección de documentos*. London: Wertheimer, Lea & Co, 1908.

Carta al Presidente Taft: en pro de la honradez internacional. London: Wertheimer, Lea & Co, 1909.

Cartas dirigidas a su primo Diego Mendoza sobre diversos asuntos [manuscrito]. Madrid, London, 1904–16.

Cartas dirigidas a su sobrino Jorge Lagos [manuscrito]. Paris, London, 1908–11.

Cuentos a Sonny. Madrid: Imprenta y Estereotipia de Ricardo Fé, 1907.

De Bogotá al Atlántico por la vía de los ríos Meta, Vichada y Orinoco. Paris: Imp. Sudamericana, 1897.

Desde lejos: (asuntos colombianos). London: Wertheimer, Lea & Co, 1907.

Desde lejos y desde cerca: (asuntos colombianos). London: Wertheimer, Lea & Co, 1909.

"Discurso de don Santiago Pérez Triana in Peregrinación a la tumba de Santiago Pérez 23 mayo 1911. Paris: Librería Paul Ollendorff, 1911, 25–27.

Down the Orinoco in a Canoe. New York: Thomas Y. Crowell, 1902.

El deber de cantar: cantos colombianos. Lausana: Imprenta Jorge Bridal, 1899.

Eslabones sueltos (asuntos colombianos). London: Wertheimer, Lea & Co, 1910.

La Casa Pérez Triana y Cia a sus relacionados. Medellín: Imprenta de El Espectador, 1890.

La Doctrina Drago: Colección de documentos. London: Wertheimer, Lea & Co, 1908.

Hispania: política, comercio, literatura, artes y ciencias 1912–16. London: Wertheimer, Lea & Co, 1912–16.

"Introducción" to Norman, Angell. *La Grande Ilusión.* Trns. S. Restrepo. Paris: Thomas Nelson and Sons, n.d.

"The Neutrality of Latin America." Address presented at the Political and Economic Circle of the National Liberal Club, February 10, 1916. London: *Hispania,* March 1, 1916, 1546–51.

"Piedras de Moler" in De la Vera del Camino. *Suplemento Literario de El Tiempo* #15 Serie II: 875

"Prólogo" in Miguel Triana, *Por el sur de Colombia: excursión pintoresco y científico al Putumayo.* Paris: Garnier Hermanos, 1907.

Reminiscencias tudescas. Bogotá: Editorial Minerva, 1936.

Some Aspects of the War. London: T. Fisher Unwin, 1915.

Tales to Sonny. London: Anthony Threherne, 1906.

The Pan-American Financial Conference of 1915. London: William Heinemann, 1915.

Una explicación. New York, 1887.

Unificación de deudas (asuntos colombianos). London: Wertheimer, Lea & Co, 1912.

III. Biographical Sketches of Santiago Pérez Triana

Cunninghame Graham, R. B. "Introduction," to *Down the Orinoco in a Canoe*. New York: Thomas Y. Crowell, 1902, viii–x.

——— "Santiago Pérez Triana." *Hispania* V:51, 1617–19.

Darío, Rubén, "Prefacio," *De Bogotá al Atlántico* 2nd Spanish Edition. Madrid, 1905.

Eastman, Tomás O. "Prólogo," in *Cuentos a Sonny*. Madrid: Imprenta y Estereotipia de Ricardo Fé, 1907, 12–15.

El Gráfico XXX, VI No. 291, June 3, 1916.

Hispania V:54, June 27, 1916.

Nieto Caballero, Luis Eduardo. *Hombres del pasado*. Bogotá: Ediciones Terra Firma Litografía Colombia, 1944.

——— "Prólogo," Santiago Pérez Triana, *Reminiscencias tudescas*. Bogotá: Tierra Firma Litografía Colombia, 1944.

Ortiz, Sergio Elías. *Santiago Pérez Triana*. Bogotá: Editorial Kelly, 1971.

Ospina, Joaquín. *Diccionario biográfico y bibliográfico de Colombia*. 3 vols. Bogotá: Editorial Águila Colombia, 1939. Vol. III, 281–82.

Quijano Wallis, José María. *Memorias: autobiográficas, historia-políticas y de carácter social*. Grottaferrata: Tipografía Italo-Orientale, 1919, 511–14.

Restrepo, A. J. "Por el Poeta," in Santiago Pérez Triana, *El deber de cantar: cantos colombianos*. Lausana: Imprenta Jorge Bridal, 1899, 1–15.

Rincón, Nemesiano. *Desde la cumbre: estudios biográficos*. Quito: Escuela Tipográfica Salesiana, 1940, 57–82.

Sanín Cano, Baldomero. *De mi vida y otros vidas*. Bogotá: Editorial ABC, 1949.

——— "Hombres que he conocido: Santiago Pérez Triana" in *Escritos*. Bogotá: Editorial Andes, 1977, 735–51.

Tellez, Hernando. "Prólogo para la edición *De Bogotá al Atlántico*. 2nd Ed. Bogotá: Biblioteca Popular de Cultura Colombiana: Editorial Kelly, 1945.

Zuleta, Eduardo. "Elogía de Santiago Pérez Triana." Leído en la Academia Colombiana el 6 de agosto de 1919. In *Anuario de la Academia Colombiana de la Lengua*. IV: 242–55. Bogotá, 1937.

IV. Other Primary Sources

Álvarez, Alejandro. *The Monroe Doctrine: Its Importance in the International Life of the States of the New World.* New York: Oxford University Press, 1924.

Pérez, Santiago, "Mensaje Presidencial" in Valencia Benavides, Hernán, ed. *Discursos y mensajes de posesión presidencial.* 2 vols. Bogotá: Imprenta Nacional, 1981, I:147–52.

Uribe, José Antonio. *Anales diplomáticos y consulares de Colombia.* 6 vols. Bogotá: Imprenta Nacional, 1918.

V. Newspapers

El Tiempo (Bogotá)
Review of Reviews (London)
The New York Times
The Times of London
The Tribune (London)

VI. Secondary Sources

Appelbaum, Nancy P. *Mapping the Country of Regions: The Chorographic Commission of Nineteenth-Century Colombia.* Chapel Hill: University of North Carolina Press, 2016.

Bassett Moore, John. "The Pan-American Financial Conferences and the Inter-American High Commission." *The American Journal of International Law* 14:3 (July 1920), 342–55.

Bergquist, Charles. *Coffee and Conflict in Colombia, 1886–1910.* Durham: Duke University Press, 1978.

Calibán, Enrique Santos Montejo. "La conflagración europea," *Danza de las horas y otros escritos*. Bogotá: Editorial Club de Lectores, 1969, 34–37.

Cataño, Gonzalo. "Mendoza Pérez, Diego," Biografías Biblioteca virtual del Banco de la Republica.

Colombia. Informe del Ministro de Relaciones Exteriores al Congreso de 1915. In Uribe, *Anales Diplomáticos*, 5: 397–555.

Conrad, Joseph. *Nostromo*. New York: Doubleday, 1960 (1904).

Correa Restrepo, Juan Santiago. "El ferrocarril de Antioquia: empresarios extranjeros y participación local," *Estudios gerenciales* April–June 2012, 28:123.

_____ *Los caminos de hierro: ferrocarriles y tranvías en Antioquia*. Bogotá: CESA, Comunicaciones, 2010.

Cruz Santos, Abel. "Economía y Hacienda Pública. De la República unitaria a la economía del medio siglo." In *Historia extensa de Colombia*. Bogotá: Editorial Lerner, 1966. Vol. XV:T.2.

Davis, Robert H. *Historical Dictionary of Colombia*. 2nd ed. Metuchen, N. J.: Scarecrow Press, 1993.

Deas, Malcolm. "Colombia, Ecuador and Venezuela, c. 1880–1930." In *Cambridge History of Latin America*, 5 vols. Cambridge: Cambridge University Press, 1984–86, 5:647.

_____ "Joseph Conrad: *Nostromo* y Colombia." In *Revista Credencial Historia* 35, November 1992.

Delpar, Helen. *Red against Blue: The Liberal Party in Colombian Politics, 1863–1899*. Tuscaloosa: University of Alabama, 1981.

Díaz Piedrahita, Santiago. *José Jerónimo Triana: naturalista multifacético*. Bogotá: Fondo Fen Colombia, 1996.

Galvis Salazar, Fernando. "Semblanza del doctor Eduardo Zuleta." *Boletín de historia y antigüedades* 51:600–02, Oct–Dec. 1964, 557–61.

Gómez Giraldo, Lucela. "Santiago Pérez Manosalbas." *Biografías Biblioteca Virtual del Banco de la República*. Accessed December 2, 2015.

Henao, Jesús María and Gerardo Arrubla. *Historia de Colombia*. Bogotá: Camacho Roldán, 1929.

Henderson, James D. *Conservative Thought in Twentieth Century Latin America: The Ideas of Laureano Gómez*. Athens: Ohio University, Monographs in International Studies Latin America Series, no. 13, 1988.

_____ *Modernization in Colombia: The Laureano Gómez Years, 1899–1965*. Gainesville: University Press of Florida, 2001.

Holguín, Jorge. *Desde cerca: asuntos colombianos*. Paris: Librairie Generale et Interntionale G. Ficker, 1908.

Horna, Hernán. "Los ferrocarriles latinoamericano del siglo XIC: el caso Colombia," in Carlos Dávila and L. de Guevara, *Empresas y empresarios en la historia de Colombia. Siglos XIX–XX: Una colección de estudios recientes*. 2 vols. Bogotá: Norma, 2003, II: 1023–44.

Mesa, Darío. "La vida política después de Panamá." In *Manual de historia de Colombia*. 3 vols. Bogotá: Instituto Colombiano de Cultura, 1978–80, III: 83–176.

Miller, J. D. B. "Norman Angell and rationality in International Relations," in D. Long and P. Wilson, eds. *Thinkers of the Twenty Years' Crisis: Inter-War Idealism Reassessed*. New York: Oxford University Press, 1995, 100–21.

Naranjo Villegas, Abel. *Generaciones colombianos*. Bogotá: El Dorado, 1976.

Ocampo López, Javier. "Centenario de Santiago Pérez: El presidente, educador y el humanista de la colombianidad." *Revista Credencial Historia*, June 2000, 126.

Palacios, Marco. *Between Legitimacy and Violence: A History of Colombia, 1875–2002*. Durham: Duke University Press, 2007.

Park, James. *Rafael Núñez and the Politics of Colombian Regionalism, 1863–1886*. Baton Rouge: Louisiana State University, 1985.

Pérez Aguirre, Antonio. *25 años de historia colombiana, 1853 a 1878, del centralismo a la federación.* Bogotá: Editorial Sucre, 1959.

Pérez, Enrique. *Vida de Felipe Pérez.* Bogotá: Imprenta de la Luz, 1911.

Pérez, Juan Manuel. "Drago Doctrine." II: 405. *Encyclopedia of Latin American History and Culture.* Ed. Barbara A. Tenenbaum. 5 vols. New York: Charles Scribner's Sons, 1996.

"Personajes del año." *Credencial Historia,* Bogotá: Vol. 175, July 2004.

Proceedings of the First Pan American Financial Conference. Washington D. C.: Government Printing Office, 1915.

Rausch, Jane. *Colombia and World War I: The Experience of a Neutral Latin American Nation during the Great War and its Aftermath, 1914–1921.* Lanham: Lexington Books, 2014.

_____ *The Llanos Frontier in Colombian History 1830–1930.* Albuquerque: University of New Mexico Press, 1993.

Rivas, Raimundo. *Historia diplomática de Colombia 1810–1934.* Bogotá: Imprenta Nacional, 1961.

Rodríguez Piñeres, Eduardo. *El olimpo radical.* Bogotá: Talleres Editoriales de Librería Voluntad, 1950.

Safford, Frank. *The Ideal of the Practical: Colombia's Struggle to Form a Technical Elite.* Austin: University of Texas, 1975.

Scarfi, Juan Pablo. "In the Name of the Americas: The Pan-American Redefinition of the Monroe Doctrine and the Emerging Language of American International Law in the Western Hemisphere, 1898–1933." *Diplomatic History* 40:2, April 2016, 189–218.

Scott, James Brown. *The Hague Peace Conferences of 1899 and 1907.* 2 vol. New York & London: Garland Publishing, 1972.

Stead, W. T. "Introduccíon," *La Doctrina Drago: colección de documentos.* London: Wertheimer, Lea & Co, 1908, lxi–lxxx.

Tschiffely, A. F. *Don Roberto: Being the Account of the Life and Works of Robert Bontine Cunninghame Graham, 1852–1936.* London: William Heinemann, 1937.

Urrutia M., Miguel and Mario Arrubla, ed. *Compendio de estadísticas históricas de Colombia.* Bogotá: National University of Colombia, 1970.

Villegas, Jorge and José Yunis, eds. *Sucesos colombianos: 1900–1924.* Medellín: Universidad de Antioquia, 1976.

Watts, Cedric. *R. B. Cunninghame Graham.* Boston: Twayne Publishers, 1983.

Watts, Cedric and Laurence Davies. *Cunninghame Graham: A Critical Biography.* New York: Cambridge University Press, 1979.

Zwicker, Lisa Fetheringill. *Dueling Students: Conflict, Masculinity, and Politics in German Universities, 1890–1915.* Ann Arbor: University of Michigan Press, 2011.

Appendix

Pérez Triana's
Best Remembered Poems

In his *Parnaso colombiano* (Medellín, n.d.), editor Hernando Salazar presents an anthology of poems written by 78 Colombian poets spanning the 19th and early 20th century. He includes only one poem penned by Santiago Pérez Triana, "Vientos del Llanos." Salazar adds that there is no printed collection of Pérez's poems, and notes that he was "a brilliant and multilingual orator" who also left dispersed the greater part of his essays and political polemics.[1]

Vientos del Llano

Tendió sus alas al viento
sobre la vasta llanura,
dilatándose en las yerbas
como caricia que ondula.
De las flexibles palmeras
en las temblosas alturas,
estremeció los penachos,
cimeras de verdes plumas.
En los recónditos senos
de la inviolada espesura,
dejó en la fronda y el nido

rumor de voces que arrullan.
De los troncos y las ramas
arrancó cadencias rudas;
son los bordones sonoros
de la agreste lira hirsuta
en que sus gritos de guerra
los huracanes modulan.
Del lago – cual ojo abierto
que su pupila profunda
refleja el sol encendido
refleja la blanca luna,
y los fantásticos sueños
que en las nubes se dibujan—
rizó las ondas azules
en florescencia de espumas.

* * *

Escaló las altas cumbres
de las montañas abruptas,
silbó entre las anchas grietas,
vibró en cavernas obscuras,
y entre los filos cortantes
de peñascos que relumbran
al rayo del sol poniente,
cual cimitarras desnudas.
Llegó hasta la excelsa cima
que la soledad circunda
y eternas nieves esmaltan
de inmaculada blancura;
ningún aliento de vida
de aquella región augusta
el soberano misterio
con su presencia conturba;
la flor, el hombre y el bruto,

vibraciones inseguras
el aroma, dolor e instinto,
que un día no más perduran,
jamás en todos los siglos,
llegaron a aquella altura;
allí tan sólo las cosas
que ley inmoral vincula
en rotación inmutable
del tiempo a la eterna fuga,
vencedora de la vida
y de la muerte fecundas;
el fulgor de las estrellas;
la claridad de la luna,
los rayos de sol que bruñen
la fulgente vestidura,
cual la cota de un guerrero
apercibido a la lucha,
y al vapor que como incienso
a la cumbre el mar tributa.

*   *   *

Como si fueran dos manos
que sobre el ara se juntan
el viento plegó las alas
sobre la cima impoluta,
sacerdote de los campos
de la selva y la llanura,
llevó el aliento de su alma
cual plegaria a las alturas,
que en blancas gasas envuelve
el incienso de las brumas.[2]

Madrid, febrero de 1904

Winds from the Plain*

The wind spread its wings
over the vast plains,
expanding across the grass
like an undulating caress.
The tufts of palm trees,
a heraldry-crest of green plumes,
shivered from
their tremulous heights.
In the remote bosom
of the untouched vegetation,
it left a rumor of lulling voices.

It plucked rough cadences
from trunks and branches
which form the sonorous bass strings
of the rugged, Hirsuta tree lyre
whose war cries
are intensified by hurricanes.

The lake, like an open eye
in whose deep pupil
the ardent sun is reflected,
the white moon is reflected,
and the fantastical dreams
which clouds sketch,
it felt the wind froth its blue waves
into a florescence of foam.

* * *

It scaled the lofty summits
of the steep mountains,
it whistled across the wide cracks,

and vibrated in the dark caves
and against the sharp-edged crags which glitter
like brandished scimitars.

It reached the topmost peak
surrounded by solitude
and glazed by everlasting snow;
no breath of life perturbed
the sovereign mystery
of that august region;
flower, man, and beast,
uncertain vibrations
of aromas, pain, and instinct,
which one day will exist no longer,
shall never reach that height
with the passing of centuries;
there exist only the things
to which the immortal rule links,
in immutable rotations,
to the time of eternal flight,
the conqueror of fecund
life and death:
the glow of the stars,
the clarity of the moon,
the sunrays which burnish
the brilliant encasing,
like a warrior's chain-mail
poised for battle,
and the mist which is like incense
offered when the sea rises.

*   *   *

As if they were two hands
which join at the altar,

the wind folded its wings
over the pristine oak tree,
priest of the fields
extending through jungle and plains,
and carried off its soul-breath
like a prayer to the great heights,
which in a white gauze
envelopes the incense smoke of the mist.

Madrid, February 1904
* English translation by Anthony Seidman

The other poem by Pérez Triana most often mentioned is "A una desconocida." As a child Luis Eduardo Nieto Caballero was enchanted by this poem and partially quoted it in his "Introducción" to Pérez Tirana's *Reminiscencias tudescas* (25–27). In *Desde la cumbre* (80–82), Nemesiano Rincón reprinted the complete version that appears below, with an epigraph by John Greenleaf Whittier.

A Una Desconocida

"Of all sad words, of tongue or pen
The saddest are these: it might have been."

I
Dicen, dicen que es digna tu hermosura
de la púrpura, el cetro y la diadema,
dicen que es tu alma virginal y pura;
que todo tu vivir es un poema.

Que es rítmico tu andar y majestuoso,
que en tu mirada hay vastos horizontes
que te envuelve en algo misterioso,
como el azul de los lejanos montes.

Que en tu redor esparces la alegría
como la encima, que la grey defiende,
su sombra, cuando el sol del mediodía
las ígneas alas sobre el mundo extiende.

Que en la ruda batalla de la vida
alta tu frente, nunca se doblega,
como el pendón de nave combatida,
que a mojarse en las ondas jamás llega.

Que el ansia de ser buena, en tu presencia
inunda el alma y de ella se apodera,
Y el ideal revive en la conciencia
Como la tierra al sol de primavera.

Que acaso sufres y que acaso lloras,
sola, incompleta, en tu misión sublime,
cual de un laúd, en las nocturnas horas,
perdida nota que en las sombras gime.

II
Por librarte de mal y de quebranto,
del dolo, del engaño y del hastío,
yo te envolviera, como en regio manto,
en el jirón de juventud que es mío.

Peregrino del Bien y de la Idea,
de lejos miro la anhelada cima,
soldado de la vida, en la pelea
combatí en todo sol y en todo clima.

Subí desde el abismo hasta las cumbres,
han sangrado mis plantas y mis manos;

he escuchado gemir las muchedumbres.
he sentido rugir los Océanos.

Del llanto y del placer oí los retos,
de la suerte sufrí las veleidades,
hay sepulcros que guardan mis secretos,
altares hay que guardan mis deidades.

Ni la envidia tenaz, ni el odio ciego
han quebrantado mi nativo brío,
conozco del verano todo el fuego,
conozco del invierno todo el frío.

Cual la hulla que guarda entre sus vetas
la luz y el fuego de extinguidos soles.
y arrancada de sus hondas grietas
nos devuelve su ardor, sus arreboles,
tal conservo del alma en lo profundo
las enseñanzas de mi hogar bendito,
que iluminan mi espíritu errabundo
entre las sombras y el dolor proscrito.

De la existencia en la penosa marcha
mi pobre corazón las guarda ufano;
como el pino del Norte entre la escarcha
la hermosa veste que le dió el verano.

Te ofrezco mi tesoro de cariño,
mi esperanza, mi fe, mis ilusiones,
te arrullaré como la madre al niño
cuando rujan deshechas las pasiones.

Abrojos no hallarás en tu sendero;
la ciencia del dolor ya me ha enseñado

a seguir del destino el derrotero:
¡sólo saben vivir los que han llorado!

III
¡Dios no lo quiere! Musa de mi lira,
eres un sueño encantador y vago,
como el eco del viento que suspira
entre las cañas que retrata el lago.

Hasta que rompa la mortal cadena
mi alma, y torne a su prístina morada
escrito está que la candente arena
azotará mi planta fatigada.

Adiós! Adiós! ensueño de un momento;
vuelve la onda al vórtice inclemente,
a su eterno soñar mi pensamiento,
a romperse entre rocas el torrente.

To A Stranger*

"Of all sad words of tongue or pen
The saddest are these: it might have been."

I
They remark that your beauty is worthy
of Tyrian purple, the scepter, and the tiara;
they remark that your soul is virginal and pure,
that your lifestyle is a poem;

that your gait is rhythmic, majestic;
that in your gaze there reside sweeping horizons
which envelope you in a nimbus
like the blueness glazing distant mountains;

that you sow joy all around you,
like the holm oak's shade sheltering the flock
when the noonday sun extends
its fiery wings over the globe;

that in the wild battle of life
you hold your head high, never falter,
like the banner of the battle ship
which will never be drenched by the waves;

that in your presences, the urge to be kind
floods one's soul, and seizes it,
and the ideal revives one's conscience,
like the earth does to the Springtime sun;

that perhaps you suffer, perhaps you weep,
alone, unaccompanied in your sublime mission,
like a lute's note which, during the nocturnal hours,
moans adrift the shadows.

II
To free you from harm and sorrow,
from deceit, from deception, and weariness,
I would envelope you with the rags of my youth
as if they were a royal cloak.

Pilgrim of Goodness and the Ideal,
from afar I gaze at the desired summit,
a soldier of life, in the struggle,
I fought in broad daylight and in every clime.

I rose from the abyss, and reached the heights;
my soles and hands have bled;

I have listened to the masses groan,
I have felt the Oceans roar.

I heard the challenges of pleasure and pain;
I suffered the whims of luck;
there are tombs that hold my secrets,
and altars that hold my deities.

Neither stubborn envy, nor blind hate
have broken my native spirit;
I know all of summer's fire,
I know all of winter's chill.

Like the brittle coal which holds
the light and fire of extinguished suns in its veins,
and when unearthed from the deep cracks
it bequeaths us its ardor, its red glow,

such is how I maintain my soul deep within,
and the teachings of my blessed home,
which illumine my wanderlust spirit
through shadows and outlawed pain.

From the laborious course of existence
my heart safe-keeps them with pride,
like the Northern pine which, covered with frost,
still glows with the beautiful garb of summer.

I offer you my treasure of kindness,
my hope, my faith, my reveries;
I will lull you to sleep like a mother does her child
When shattered passions roar.

You will find no thorns on your path;
the lessons of pain have already taught me
to follow the trail's ending;
only those who have wept know how to live!

III
God does not wish it to be so! Muse of my lyre
you are an enchanting, nebulous dream,
like the wind's echo which sighs
among the reeds reflected in the lake.

Until my soul breaks
from the mortal chain, and returns to its original dwelling,
it is inscribed that the burning sand
will lash at my weary soles.

Farewell! Farewell! A moment's flight of fancy;
the wave returns to the violent whirlpool,
and my thoughts to their eternal dream,
dashed among the torrent's crags.

*English translation by Anthony Seidman

Index

www.ingramcontent.com/pod-product-compliance
Lightning Source LLC
Chambersburg PA
CBHW020611270326
41927CB00005B/274